LIGHTS CAMERA BOOZE

LIGHTS CAMERA BOOZE

Drinking Games
for Your Favorite Movies

Written by Kourtney Jason & Lauren Metz

Illustrated by Amanda Lanzone

Ulysses Press

Published by:
Ulysses Press
P.O. Box 3440
Berkeley, CA 94703
www.ulyssespress.com

ISBN: 978-1-61243-238-0
Library of Congress Control Number: 2013938282

Printed in the United States by Bang Printing

10 9 8 7 6 5 4 3 2 1

Acquisitions Editor: Keith Riegert
Managing Editor: Claire Chun
Editor: Lauren Harrison
Proofreader: Elyce Berrigan-Dunlop
Cover design: Amanda Lanzone
Interior design and layout: Jake Flaherty

Distributed by Publishers Group West

A huge thank you to the oh-so-creative minds at Ulysses Press, whose energy and enthusiasm helped us shape this book into the best addition to a party since the invention of the red Solo cup.

To our friends and family, hugs for your love and support. We eagerly look forward to playing a game or two or thirty-three with you.

Now, everyone, please raise your glasses. To you! Two great friends had a blast writing this book hoping it'd lead to you and your crew making hilarious new memories together. (You know, the ones you can actually remember.)

Cheers!
Kourtney and Lauren

TABLE OF CONTENTS

INTRODUCTION

Movies are so much better with booze.

Libations and cinema come together in *Lights Camera Booze*, where you'll find drinking games for all your favorite movies in one awesome place (this book, duh).

Featuring 33 movies released throughout the past four decades (hey, just like a fine wine, the movies from 1975 get better with age!), *Lights Camera Booze* will transform any regular ol' movie night into a superfun party—but don't blame us if parts of the magical evening become a little hazy.

Flip through the book and you'll find a variety of movies for all kinds of cinema tastes. We've got movies you loved from your childhood or teenage years (*The Goonies*, *The Princess Bride*, *Scream*), instant classics of the last decade (*Mean Girls*, *Anchorman*, *Magic Mike*), and the flicks you can watch over and over and over again (*Fight Club*, *Office Space*, *Legally Blonde*).

Each movie drinking game consists of five elements:

1. A movie-themed suggested cocktail (with recipe) to imbibe during the game
2. Two pages of drinking game rules with illustrations
3. Jaw-dropping trivia
4. Movie-related questions to ask your friends post-movie watching (you'll learn new secrets about your pals!)
5. And a final challenge to see who can best hold their liquor!

Take a look through the book and pick which movie you'll screen for your friends. Be sure to read through the whole game prior to the party, since some games require props for the final challenge. You'll also need to know what booze and ingredients to pick up for the cocktails.

Before you watch the movie, go over the drinking game rules with everyone. When it's time to drink based on the rules provided, only take sips—do not chug your drink! We repeat, do not chug your drink. You can also divide the rules among you and your friends. Split into two teams, with each team assigned to only the even or odd numbered rules. Or assign each player one or two rules, and they will only sippy-sip to those.

The book is intended to lie flat on your coffee table and the rules are drawn big enough to see from most angles. Plus, it'll give you a chance to glance down if you happen to forget a few.

We also suggest which rules to omit if you're a light drinker. Getting drunk with your friends is fun. Becoming the asshole who can't take care of themselves and doesn't know when to stop drinking is not fun. Just a friendly reminder from your drinking game goddesses.

Bottoms up!

AMERICAN PIE

There's nothing quite like your first time. It's just so awkward! But no matter how bad, weird, or short it was, you always want to do it again. And is there anything more hilarious than a group of high school boys with raging hormones making a pact to lose their V-cards by prom night?

American Pie was one of the first movies to take the high school comedy to a new level of raunch, gross-out humor, and embarrassing sexcapades. Take Jimbo (Jason Biggs), who gets caught masturbating by his parents, busts a nut too quickly (twice! And while it's being broadcast across the web!), and ends up getting used for sex on prom night—which actually is kind of cool.

American Pie lets you laugh (and drink!) at other people's sexual misfortunes, while also allowing you to pretend these embarrassing moments have never happened to you.

Note: *If you're a light drinker, skip rules 12 and 18.*

DRINK OF THE GAME

KEG O' BEER

A pony keg serves approximately 60 (16-ounce) beers. A regular keg serves about 125 (16-ounce) beers. Purchase accordingly. And make sure you're drinking a jizz-free beer.

Put the keg on ice. Tap it. Pump it. Pour into a red Solo cup. Drink. Repeat.

DRINK WHEN...

1. STIFLER SAYS SOMETHING DOUCHEY

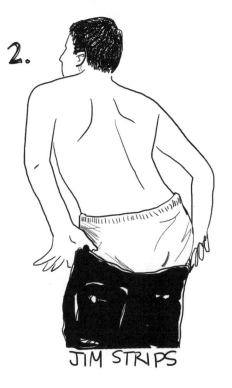

2.

JIM STRIPS

3. FAMOUS ROCK BAND CAMEO

4. M.I.L.F.

5. SEXUAL INNUENDOS

6. SOMEONE WALKS IN ON JIM

7. "VIRGIN"

8. STIFLER'S MOM

9. UNDERAGE DRINKING

10. BAND CAMP STORIES: "THIS ONE TIME..."

11. "SUCK ME, BEAUTIFUL."

12. SOMEONE SAYS SHERMAN'S (AKA SHERMINATOR'S) NAME

14. OZ SINGS ♫

13. APPLE PIE

15. RUMORS SPREAD ABOUT FINCH

16. MASTURBATION

17.

18. ANYONE SAYS

TRIVIA

SAUSAGE FEST

What did the crew cook, stick on a pencil, wrap in aluminum foil, and then place between Jason Biggs's legs? Yup, it was a sausage! To replicate an erection, in fact. And the meat was still warm when it was put in place.

TOO CRUDE, TOO LEWD

It took four edits to get the film an R-rating instead of NC-17.

MS. AMERICAN PIE

The pie Jim violates wasn't actually homemade. It was from Costco.

CERVEZA CON JIZZ

The brewski Stifler drinks is actually beer with egg whites in it, a concoction that would still make us vomit.

QUOTE IT

In the sex scene between Jim and Michelle, Alyson Hannigan ad-libbed the line, "Say my name, bitch." Everyone found it hilarious that it was kept in the final cut.

HOT TOPICS

1. *Tell us about your first time.*
2. *What has been the most awkward sexual moment in all of your life?*

FAKING IT

Everyone is guilty of faking an orgasm at least once. Let's see who's the champion of faking it. To decide the order of performances, have each person draw a number out of a hat. Start with the person who drew number 1. Each person gets 30 seconds to give their best fake orgasm. Each person can earn a score between 1 (you call that your O face?!) and 5 (wait, are you sure you were just faking it?!). The faker with the highest score wins.

ANCHORMAN:
THE LEGEND OF RON BURGUNDY

Sixty percent of the time, you'll love this game every time. Ron Burgundy and his mishmash team of misogynists run Channel 4 News like a middle-aged frat. . .that is, until the sultry Veronica Corningstone comes in and knocks them off their boys-club-only pedestals.

Keep an eye out for A-list cameos from Seth Rogen as the eager KVWN cameraman and Ben Stiller as leader of Spanish Language News. And, of course, raise your glass to vindictive biker Jack Black (Baxterrrr!) and lead anchor Luke Wilson, whose Channel 2 news team ranks third in the ratings. Sorry, Luke.

And good news for all you *Anchorman* fanatics. The movie's long-awaited sequel, *Anchorman: The Legend Continues* has Kristen Wiig joining the cast as Brick's wife and features cameos from Tina Fey, Amy Poehler, and more.

Until then, you stay classy, San Diego.

Note: *If you're a light drinker, skip rules 4, 7, and 13.*

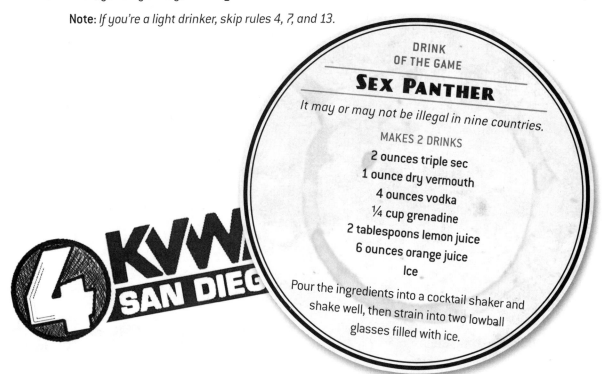

DRINK
OF THE GAME

SEX PANTHER

It may or may not be illegal in nine countries.

MAKES 2 DRINKS

2 ounces triple sec
1 ounce dry vermouth
4 ounces vodka
¼ cup grenadine
2 tablespoons lemon juice
6 ounces orange juice
Ice

Pour the ingredients into a cocktail shaker and shake well, then strain into two lowball glasses filled with ice.

DRINK WHEN...

1. RON ROCKS A TURTLENECK

2. TELEPROMPTER

3. SOMEONE'S TIE

4. IS **TOO SHORT**

5. THE NARRATOR SPEAKS

6. ANIMAL-FOCUSED NEWS STORY

7. SAN DIEGO

8. "WHEN IN ROME"

9. BRICK SAYS SOMETHING ⟶ KIND OF **STUPID**

10. NEWS TEAMS ARGUE

11. SOMEONE TAKES A DRINK 🥃

12. **RON INCORRECTLY STATES A FACT**

13.

14. SOMEONE HITS ON VERONICA CORNINGSTONE

15. WES MANTOOTH

16.

17. CAMEOS FROM:
   JACK BLACK, LUKE WILSON
   BEN STILLER, OR SETH ROGEN

HOT TOPICS

1. What's the best one-liner in the film? (Tough one, we know!)
2. Of all the news teams, which anchor would you sleep with?

TRIVIA

TIME TRAVEL

Although set in the 1970s, many items featured in the movie weren't invented until years later. Examples? The lint roller used on Ron's blazer and the pepper spray shown during his fight with Veronica. Also, scenes of San Diego include Petco Park, which didn't open until April 2004.

EXTRA! EXTRA!

So many extra scenes were filmed that *Wake Up, Ron Burgundy: The Lost Movie* was edited and packaged with the two-disc *Anchorman: Special Edition*.

LEADING NEWS LADY

Jake's sis Maggie Gyllenhaal auditioned to play Veronica.

SPECIAL REPORT

Pass everyone a piece of paper and a pen. Then give everyone five minutes to write a news story about what they did last weekend. Go around in a circle reporting the news, and the most entertaining story wins.

NATIONAL LAMPOON'S ANIMAL HOUSE

Toga! Toga! This 1978 comedy classic introduced the world to Kevin Bacon, and "Shout" was never the same.

Today, many a generation has rocked Bluto's "College" T-shirt, but not everyone in the cast believed in the film's golden potential. An unimpressed Donald Sutherland was offered either $75,000 (for three days of work!) or a percentage of the gross. He chose the former, and the decision cost him $3 to $4 million—ouch!

But Kiefer Sutherland's pops still went on to enjoy regal pastures, playing the cold-hearted President Snow in *The Hunger Games*. And, well, who cares if he doubted *Animal House*'s potential anyway? Roger Ebert gave the flick his seal of approval back in '78, and we still feel the same today.

Note: *If you're a light drinker, skip rules 5 and 12.*

DRINK OF THE GAME

THE TOGATINI

Smashing the glass after you've finished is optional.

MAKES 2 DRINKS

4 ounces vanilla vodka

12 ounces ginger ale

Ice

Mix and serve chilled in two lowball glasses with ice.

DRINK WHEN...

1. A GIRL WEARS A BRA

2. KATY NAGS BOON

3. OLDIES MUSIC PLAYS

4. YOU SEE GREEK LETTERS

5. PLAID CLOTHES

6.

COLLEGE

7. KEVIN BACON

8. SOMETHING BREAKS

9. SOMEONE'S **DRUNK**

10. DEAN WORMER PLOTS AGAINST **DELTA**

11. SOMEONE WEARS A **PLEDGE PIN**

12. "**DELTA**"

13. CAR CRASH

15. "OMEGA"

14.  PROFESSOR JENNINGS

16. **FRONT** OF THE **DELTA HOUSE**

TRIVIA

ART IMITATING LIFE

Cowriter Chris Miller based the National Lampoon short stories, from which the movie was a spinoff, on his real-life good ol' times as an Alpha Delta Phi frat boy at Dartmouth.

BELIEVE IT OR NOT!

Toga parties only became a college staple after the release of this movie.

WIPEOUT

The dilapidated 1800s home used for Delta's exterior shots was torn down in the '80s.

SWITCHEROO

Delta changes from Delta Chi Tau to Delta Tau Chi during the movie.

BACK TO THE FUTURE

Fact: We're about as far removed from 1985 as Marty McFly was from 1955. Scary thought, right? So is the image of a teenage version of your mom having the hots for you. Chills.

Still, this film remains a legend—as does Doc's DeLorean—and it spawned two additional movies: one that includes a trip to 2015 (we're pretty much there, so why can't cars fly yet?) and the final chapter of this trilogy, which rewinds to 1885.

If the concept of time travel isn't mind-blowing enough for you, how about finding out that Michael J. Fox's middle name isn't John. Or Joseph. Or Jeremy. Or Jacob. Or any other J name. Nope, it's Andrew. So where's the J come from? It's a salute to actor Michael J. Pollard.

Why the switch? The '80s heartthrob feared that sticking to his real name would result in teen magazines running the headline "Michael, A Fox!" Good call there, Michael Andrew.

Note: *If you're a light drinker, skip rules 4, 7, and 11.*

DRINK OF THE GAME

THE DOCQUIRI

Fortunately, plutonium isn't a crucial ingredient.

MAKES 2 DRINKS

3 ounces light rum
2 ounces fresh lime juice
2 teaspoons simple syrup
Lime wedges, for garnish

Pour the rum, lime juice, and simple syrup into a cocktail shaker and shake well. Strain into two chilled martini glasses. Garnish each with a lime wedge.

DRINK WHEN...

1. 1985

2. SKATEBOARDS =MARTY—

3. MARTY DRIVES THE DeLOREAN

4. TIME IS SHOWN

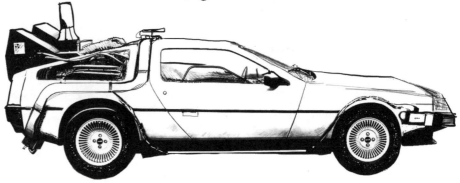

5. MARTY —OR— DOC FLIPS A SWITCH —OR— TURNS ON A MACHINE

6. DOC HELPS MARTY

7. "McFLY"

8. SOMEONE TALKS ABOUT MARTY'S CLOTHES

9. MARTY DOES OR SAYS SOMETHING FROM THE FUTURE

10. BIFF

11. "TIME"

12. LORRAINE *Flirts* WITH MARTY

13. 1955

14. THE OLD → CLOCK TOWER

15. PLUTONIUM

16. MARTY PUSHES GEORGE TO ASK OUT LORRAINE

TRIVIA

ROLE REVERSAL

Can you imagine *Back to the Future* without Michael J. Fox? It almost happened after he gave up the role due to scheduling conflicts with *Family Ties*. Eric Stoltz was then cast as Marty McFly, but after a few weeks, it was decided that he wasn't a fit and Michael was approached again. Ultimately, to balance playing both Marty and Alex P. Keaton, Fox filmed the movie after tapings of the show. Let's just say he didn't get much sleep for a while.

GEMINI BABIES

Lea Thompson, who plays Marty's mom, is only ten days older than Michael J. Fox.

WELL PLAYED, SPIELBERG

When Universal Pictures head Sid Sheinberg wrote a memo about changing the film's name to *Spaceman from Pluto*—because he felt no one would see a movie with "future" in the title—Steven Spielberg responded by thanking him for the "joke memo" that everyone loved. As hoped, Sheinberg dropped the idea instead of admitting that he truly wanted the change.

HOUSEHOLD NAME

Marty's mom is named Lorraine after Sheinberg's wife.

HOT TOPICS

1. *If you possessed the power to time travel, when and where would you go?*

2. *If you could go back in time and do something differently, what would you change?*

ROCK OUT

Stand in a circle and go around naming '80s singers and bands. You can't repeat what someone has already said or take more than three seconds to shout out your answer. Once you're out, you sit for the rest of the game and the last person standing is the winner.

THE BIG LEBOWSKI

This is not 'Nam. This is *The Big Lebowski* drinking game, man. And there are rules if you want to live the life of a Dude who's just trying to take it easy. It's so fuckin' simple, Donny could do it. So grab your White Russian, slip on your jellies, relax in your robe, and hold onto your toes. But don't let anyone piss on your carpet—it really pulls the room together.

Whether you're a dude or a dudette, this game is for true fans of the cult film. Despite being a disappointment at the box office in 1998, *The Big Lebowski* has only grown in popularity, having spawned a religion, a store in NYC, and multiple annual festivals paying tribute to the flick. Now it's up to you and your friends to hang with the Dude, Walter, and Donny. The question is: Will you abide?

Note: *If you're a light drinker, skip rule 1.*

DRINK OF THE GAME

WHITE RUSSIAN

Too many, and you might be the one pissing on your rug. Abide responsibly.

MAKES 2 DRINKS

4 ounces vodka

2 ounces Kahlúa

Ice

2 ounces heavy cream

Pour vodka and Kahlúa over ice in an old fashioned glass. Stir. Top with cream.

→ DRINK WHEN...

1. EL DUDERINO REFERS TO HIMSELF IN THE **3RD PERSON**

2. THE DUDE (SMOKES) POT

3. ANYONE BOWLS A **STRIKE**

4. WALTER MENTIONS **VIETNAM**

5. HIS DUDENESS DRINKS A **WHITE RUSSIAN**

6.

SHUT THE FUCK UP, DONNY!

7.

8. **FERRET!**

9. ANY MENTION OF THE RUG

10. MAUDE SAYS "VAGINA"

11. SOMEONE TALKS ABOUT A "JOHNSON"

12. A CERTAIN U.S. PRESIDENT APPEARS

13. 🔲 "THIS IS WHAT HAPPENS WHEN YOU FUCK A STRANGER IN THE ASS!"

14.

15. SOMETHING IS USED AS A WEAPON

DE JESUS

16. NIHILISTS

17. THE DUDE WEARS JELLIES

TRIVIA

CENSORING GONE WRONG

The edited-for-TV version of *The Big Lebowski* changes Walter's line, "This is what happens when you fuck a stranger in the ass," to something a bit more tame: "This is what happens when you find a stranger in the Alps!" Not quite the same effect.

FUCKIN' DUDE COUNT

"Dude" is said a total of 160 times during the movie. And it shows up once as text in the credits for "Gutterballs," Lebowski's dream sequence. "Fuck," or a derivative of it, is said 292 times in the movie. And "man" counts in at 147. (But we didn't tally those ourselves. We trusted the web.)

CHUG-A-LUG

"Careful, man, there's a beverage here!" The Dude imbibes nine White Russians and spills one at Jackie Treehorn's mansion.

PACKING HEAT

Is there something in your pants, or are you just happy to see me? The Jesus's ridiculously large bulge is actually a large bag of bird seed shoved down his pants.

NOT A GOLFER

The Dude loves bowling. But you never once see him bowl.

HOT TOPICS

1. *Would you rather sleep with Walter or Jesus? Would you rather sleep with Bunny or Maude?*

2. *Have you ever been mistaken for someone else?*

SLURRING YOUR WORDS, MAN?

You've had a few White Russians. Now's the time to see who's got the skills for this tongue twister. One player will start by saying "Shomer Shabbos" five times fast. Go around the room and have each person take a turn. The key to winning is to not slur your words.

THE
BREAKFAST CLUB

Detention never seemed so, well, not that bad. This quintessential coming-of-age John Hughes film (of *Ferris Bueller's Day Off* and *Sixteen Candles* fame) begins on a chilly Saturday morning and ends with five high school students each making a personal breakthrough.

From bonding over their crappy parents to getting high together to pass the time, somehow the princess begins to tolerate the criminal and the basket case finally speaks (33 minutes into the movie to be exact, according to IMDB). Off-screen, the cast was part of the iconic '80s "Brat Pack" that held Hollywood in the palm of its young and super-rich hands.

You may have missed your chance to join this exclusive group and party with a young Emilio Estevez and Molly Ringwald, but this game is the next best thing.

Note: *If you're a light drinker, skip rules 2, 3, 8, and 13.*

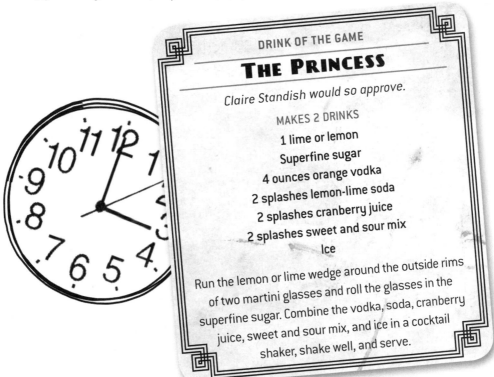

DRINK OF THE GAME

THE PRINCESS

Claire Standish would so approve.

MAKES 2 DRINKS

1 lime or lemon
Superfine sugar
4 ounces orange vodka
2 splashes lemon-lime soda
2 splashes cranberry juice
2 splashes sweet and sour mix
Ice

Run the lemon or lime wedge around the outside rims of two martini glasses and roll the glasses in the superfine sugar. Combine the vodka, soda, cranberry juice, sweet and sour mix, and ice in a cocktail shaker, shake well, and serve.

DRINK WHEN...

1. ANDREW TALKS ABOUT WRESTLING

2. YOU SEE A CLOCK

3. BENDER PISSES SOMEONE OFF

4.

C
A
R
L

5. "VERNON"

6. °° VIRGIN °°

7. BENDER GETS ANOTHER DETENTION

8. SOMEONE SHARES SOMETHING PERSONAL

9. SOMEONE TALKS ABOUT A PARENT

10. SOMEONE STARES AT ALLISON

11. SOMEONE TALKS ABOUT WHY THEY'RE IN DETENTION

#12. SOMEONE LEAVES THE LIBRARY

DETENTION SLIP

#13. STEREOTYPING

14. VERNON THREATENS ONE OF THEM

15.  SOMEONE MENTIONS OR SMOKES POT

16. BENDER SHOVES OR BREAKS SOMETHING

#7. "DON'T YOU FORGET ABOUT ME" PLAYS

TRIVIA

BEHIND-THE-SCENES DRAMA

John Cusack was first slated to play Bender, but he was later replaced by Judd Nelson, who was rumored to butt heads off-camera with both Molly Ringwald and John Hughes.

SCRIPT SWAP

Emilio Estevez was also set to play Bender, but after producers failed to fill Andrew's role, he agreed to take on the part. Similarly, Molly Ringwald was originally considered to play Allison, but eventually convinced John Hughes she was a better Claire.

FAST ONE

John Hughes wrote the movie's screenplay in just two days.

NEVER HAVE I EVER: HIGH SCHOOL EDITION

Sit in a circle and take turns, each person beginning a sentence with "In high school, never have I ever…" and finishing with something you did (or didn't do). For example, "In high school, never have I ever stolen my parents' car for a night." Raise your glass and take a sip if you did—first person to finish their drink wins!

HOT TOPICS

1. *What's the craziest thing you did that landed you in detention?*
2. *What were you in high school and what are you now: a princess, a jock, a brain, a criminal, or a basket case?*

BRING IT ON

Raise your hand if you say "burr" and immediately think "it's cold in here." You are not alone, my friend.

In this film, Kirsten Dunst finds herself dealing with a complete cheertastrophe after learning her squad ripped off the Clovers' routine. The cheer horror. Desperate times call for desperate measures, people, and thus "spirit fingers" entered our vocabularies.

Now let's salute this high-flying hit that lead to four (or 40) additional *Bring It On* movies and even a Broadway musical. Cheers!

Note: *If you're a light drinker, skip rules 14 and 15.*

DRINK OF THE GAME

THE CHERRY CHEERTINI

Don't even think about sharing this recipe with the competition.

MAKES 2 DRINKS

2 ounces cherry vodka
2 ounces cherry schnapps
6 ounces lemon-lime soda
Maraschino cherries, for garnish

Combine the vodka, schnapps, and soda in a cocktail shaker and stir well. Serve in two chilled glasses. Top each drink with two maraschino cherries.

DRINK WHEN...

1. ANY MENTION OF NATIONALS

2. SPIRIT STICK

3. CHEER FIGHT!

4. AARON ACTS LIKE AN ASS

5. SOMEONE SAYS "EAST COMPTON"

6. ↘ "GO TOROS!"

7. "SPIRIT FINGERS"

8. SOMEONE DOES A CARTWHEEL

9. BIG RED

10. A FOOTBALL PLAYER MOCKS A **MALE CHEERLEADER**

11. COURTNEY UNDERMINES TORRANCE'S **CHEERTHORITY**

12. SOMEONE MAKES A **CHEER PUN**

13. CLIFF AND MISSY TRADE INSULTS

14. ♡ **CLIFF** ➜

15. CLOVERS UNIFORM

16. TORRANCE ≡ FIGHTS ≡ WITH HER **BRO**

17. TORRANCE GIVES THE SQUAD A **PEP TALK**

TRIVIA

BEEN THERE, DONE THAT

Sure enough, both Kirsten Dunst and Gabrielle Union cheered in high school.

FAMILIAR TUNE

When Missy yells out the hotel's window, the cheer she hears belongs to Kirsten Dunst's high school alma mater.

LET ME HEAR IT

Three Clover cheerleaders—Lava (Shamari Fears), Jenelope (Natina Reed), and Lafred (Brandi Williams)—are real-life members of the band Blaque and sing "As If" on the soundtrack.

HOT TOPICS

1. *Who was your rival in high school? What's the worst thing you did to each other?*

2. *If you put together a squad, what would you name it?*

GIVE ME A...

It's cheer-off time! Designate one person as the judge and divide the room into two squads. Start the clock! Each team has ten minutes to come up with a cheer and routine. Bonus points for splits.

CLERKS

Who knew a day in the lives of two convenience store clerks could be so hilariously inappropriate, leave you in complete and utter shock thanks to a darkened bathroom rendezvous, and launch a decades-long career for a filmmaker from Jersey?

Clerks is Kevin Smith's full-length directorial debut—and it's often still considered his best film to date. Following employees Dante and Randal as they insult customers, play hockey on the roof, and debate the most important of topics (*Jedi* vs. *Empire Strikes Back*, best ways to count the number of your sexual partners), *Clerks* nails the art of fast-paced, witty dialogue that carries a movie about nothing.

The film had a budget of just over $27,000 and was financed almost entirely by Smith via maxed-out credit cards, profits from selling a majority of his comic book collection, and borrowed cash-ola from friends and family. It was a wise investment as *Clerks* grossed more than $3 million in the U.S. and put Kevin Smith on the ol' Hollywood map. Sure beats working in Quick Stop, doesn't it?

Note: *If you're a light drinker, skip rule 4.*

DRINK OF THE GAME

FADE-ORADE

Dante: "So who's going to pay for all those Gatorades?"
Sanford: "What do you care, you shoe-polish-smelling motherfucker?"

MAKES 4 TO 6 DRINKS

1 (32-ounce) bottle chilled fruit punch flavored Gatorade

10 ounces chilled vodka

Mix the Gatorade and vodka together in a pitcher. Stir, then serve.

DRINK WHEN...

1. DANTE SAYS, "I'M NOT EVEN SUPPOSED TO BE HERE TODAY!"

2. RANDAL CLOSES RST VIDEO

3. DANTE WHINES ABOUT ANYTHING

4. JAY & SILENT BOB

5. SOMEONE WANTS TO BUY CIGARETTES

6. DANTE CLOSES Quick STOP

7. RANDAL MAKES A SLURPING NOISE

8. A CUSTOMER ASKS,

"ARE YOU OPEN?"

9. ANYONE TALKS ABOUT

CAITLIN

10. CHAPTER TITLES FLASH ON SCREEN

11.  HOCKEY REFERENCES ARE MADE

12. STAR WARS

13. "SHOE POLISH"

14. JAY DANCES

15. HANDMADE STORE SIGNS

TRIVIA

TRUE LIFE

Clerks was filmed at the same store where Kevin Smith was working at the time. They shot for 21 continuous nights. Smith's store shifts would start at 6 a.m. and end at 11 p.m. Then, they'd shoot until 4 a.m. so that Smith could still get an hour or two of sleep before starting it all over again.

CANDID CAMERA

Jason Mewes (Jay) was extremely camera shy and couldn't film his dance scene if everyone was watching him. To calm Jason's nerves, the crew stood in the video store while the cameras rolled and filmed the scene.

CUM AGAIN

Randal and the *Happy Scrappy Hero Pup* mom did not film their scene together. Actor Jeff Anderson refused to read the list of porn movie titles in front of her and the child actor. However, to get the appropriate reaction shots of the mom, the list of movie titles was read aloud to her.

COLLAGE TIME

The *Clerks* logo is made from letters cut out of various magazines and food items. The C is from *Cosmopolitan* magazine, the L is from *Life*, the E is from *Rolling Stone*, the R is from Ruffles potato chips, the K is from a Clark Bar, and the S is from a Goobers box.

I OBJECT

Clerks was originally rated NC-17 by the MPAA based entirely on its heavy use of curse words. Miramax, the film's distributor, hired attorney Alan M. Dershowitz (of the O.J. Simpson defense team), who got the MPAA to lower its rating to R without any cuts.

HOT TOPICS

1. *Would you rather have a partner who's slept with 12 other people or gone down on 36 other people?*

2. *Which is better:* Return of the Jedi *or* The Empire Strikes Back*?*

TABLE HOCKEY TOURNAMENT

To play, you will need two pots and one deck of cards. Two players will play at a time. Split the deck in half, giving each player 26 cards. Players will sit at opposing ends of a long table with a pot in front of them. Take turns throwing one card at a time into your opponent's pot. The player with the most cards in their opponent's pot wins and moves on to the next round. Continue the matches until one person proves victorious.

CLUELESS

Ugh, as if...there's any other classic and quotable teen movie worthy of a drinking game as much as *Clueless*. The 1995 flick (yup, that makes us feel old) stands the test of time as one of the best teen comedies ever made. Life just wouldn't be the same without this movie. Like, can you even remember a day when "As if!" and "Whatever!" weren't a part of your vocab?

Clueless also taught us that "Rollin' with the Homies" is a great song and an even better dance move, that *Ren & Stimpy* are "way existential," and that you don't want to be a "Monet" like Amber (Hagsville!). Now, don't bug. Let's cheers to *Clueless* and our favorite matchmaking virgin who can't drive, Cher.

Note: *If you're a light drinker, skip rule 2.*

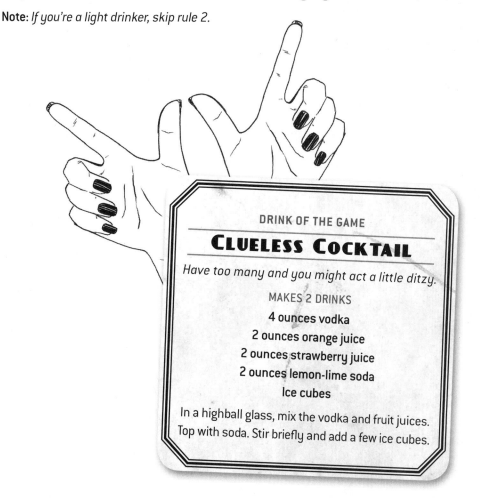

DRINK OF THE GAME

CLUELESS COCKTAIL

Have too many and you might act a little ditzy.

MAKES 2 DRINKS

4 ounces vodka
2 ounces orange juice
2 ounces strawberry juice
2 ounces lemon-lime soda
Ice cubes

In a highball glass, mix the vodka and fruit juices. Top with soda. Stir briefly and add a few ice cubes.

*DRINK WHEN...

1. "AS IF!"

2. CHER'S VOICEOVER

3. MAKEOVER MONTAGE

4.  "YOU'RE A VIRGIN WHO CAN'T DRIVE!"

5. ♪ Rollin' with the homies ♪

6.  WHATEVER

7. CHER PLAYS MATCH MAKER

8. ANYONE TALKS ABOUT SEX

9. SKATEBOARDS

10. CHER NEGOTIATES HER GRADES

11. CHER INSULTS AMBER

12.

PLAID MINISKIRTS

13. CRANBERRIES C.D.

14. CHER PULLS A HIT AND RUN

15. MR. HOROWITZ YELLS

16. Hair Flip

17. CHER TALKS FASHION

18. SOMEONE -SAYS- "CLUELESS"

TRIVIA

GO WITH IT
Alicia Silverstone is a bit *Clueless* herself! In the scene when she gives a speech comparing Haiti to her father's dinner party, she incorrectly pronounces "Haitians." Director Amy Heckerling didn't correct Alicia because the mess-up fit in so perfectly with Cher's personality.

MAD FOR PLAID
There are 53 different kinds of tartan/plaid used in the film; 7 are worn by Cher and 12 by other major characters.

SUCK AND BLOW

Just like Spin the Bottle, Suck and Blow is a classic party game to play with your crush. You just might finally kiss! But you'll also want to be careful in choosing the players for the game. First, get a deck of cards; you need just one card to play. Organize the players into a straight line or a circle. Anyone can start the game by putting the card to their lips and inhaling to keep the card attached to their mouth. This person will put their face up close to the person standing next to them. They will exhale while the second person inhales. This passes the card from person to person. If you're receiving the card you suck, and when you're giving it away you blow. If the card falls down between two players, they have to kiss. Pucker up!

HOT TOPICS

1. Are you like Cher, Dionne, or Tai?

2. Describe the outfit you're most embarrassed you ever wore.

3. Predict your life as a grown-up with this Clueless-themed MASH (Mansion, Apartment, Shack, House) game. Use the following answers for the different categories:
   A. **Boys** (Josh, Murray, Travis, Elton)
   B. **Career** (Fashion Designer, Lawyer, Teacher)
   C. **Car** (White Jeep, Red Convertible, 1954 Nash Metropolitan)
   D. **City** (Paris, NYC, Beverly Hills)
   E. **Report Card Grades** (As, Bs, Cs);
   F. **Number of Kids** (0, 1, 2, 5)
   G. **Wedding Dress Designer** (Azzedine Alaia, Calvin Klein, Fred Segal)

To Play *Grab a blank page of paper, and draw a box in the center of it. Write MASH at the top and the categories and answers around the center box. Have a friend draw tally marks in the box until you say, "Stop." Count the lines. Start with the M in MASH and continue counting each answer. When you reach the number of tally marks, cross out that answer. Skip any eliminated answers as you continue counting, until one answer is left in each category.*

DIRTY DANCING

If you didn't have a crush on Patrick Swayze after watching *Dirty Dancing*, you belong in a playpen with Baby! His skintight shirts. His thick hair that you just want to run your fingers through. His smoldering gaze. And the way those hips move. It's easy to see why Baby was swooning over him.

Though it was released in 1987, *Dirty Dancing* was a favorite of many girls in the '90s. We all dreamed of having a summer romance like Baby and Johnny (but, you know, without the pregnant friend and back-alley abortion). We mainly just wanted to passionately dance with a guy as handsome as Johnny. It really would have been the time of our lives.

Note: *If you're a light drinker, skip rule 9.*

DRINK
OF THE GAME

WATERMELON BELLINI

"I carried a watermelon." Oh Baby, could there have been anything worse to say the first time you met Johnny?

MAKES 8 DRINKS

3 cups cubed, seeded watermelon, frozen
2 tablespoons sugar
2 tablespoons fresh lemon juice
3 cups chilled Prosecco or sparkling wine, divided

In a blender, combine the watermelon, sugar, lemon juice, and 1 cup sparkling wine. Process until smooth. Pour ⅓ cup watermelon mixture into each of the eight champagne flutes. Pour about ¼ cup of the remaining sparkling wine into each glass.

DRINK WHEN...

1. PELVISES COLLIDE
2. SOMEONE EXHIBITS CLA$$I$T BEHAVIOR

3. LINE DANCING
4. ANYONE PLAYS CARDS
5. SEINFELD'S NEWMAN
6. BABY SAYS "DADDY"
7. BABY DANCES ALONE OR BADLY
8. VOICES HEARD ON THE LOUDSPEAKER

9. ANYONE DANCING DOES A **BACKBEND**

WATERMELONS

10.

11. "KELLERMAN'S"

12. PREGNANCY IS REFERRED TO AS "TROUBLE"

13. LISA SINGS

14. "NOBODY PUTS BABY IN THE CORNER"

JOHNNY LIFTS ⟵ 15. BABY

16. LISA TALKS ABOUT ROBBIE

TRIVIA

TICKLE MONSTER

In the dance scene where Johnny and Baby are practicing, she keeps laughing when he runs his arm down hers. Her giggle and his frustration were both genuine emotions as those reactions were not written into the scene.

IN TROUBLE

Dirty Dancing was set in 1963, when abortion was still illegal in the U.S. It's never explicitly stated what medical procedure Penny needed, but it was an illegal, back-alley abortion, and the scenario was similar to what many women seeking abortions experienced at the time.

LOOKS CAN BE DECEIVING

Jennifer Grey was 27 when she auditioned for the role of Baby, who was just 17 and fresh out of high school. To land the role, she had to prove she could play ten years younger and that she had the dance skills needed.

HOT TOPICS

1. *Have you ever dated or hooked up with someone your parents disliked?*
2. *When was the first time you ever dirty danced with someone?*

HOW LOW CAN YOU GO?

It's time for the LIMBO! You will need a pole, yard stick, closet rack, or other long, sturdy rod for this game. The pole will be held parallel to the ground by two people. Players will form a line and attempt to pass under the bar by doing a backbend. With each round, the bar is lowered an inch or two. Players are disqualified when they fall over, touch the bar, or can't completely clear the bar. The last player remaining wins!

FERRIS BUELLER'S DAY OFF

Ferris Bueller, can you be our best friend?

The epitome of Mr. Popular, everyone from police officers to freshmen want to "Save Ferris" upon hearing he's (cough) sick (cough). Well, almost everyone. Jeanie would rather expose her brother for skipping school than spend her summer dancing with Johnny Castle. Oh, wait. Wrong '80s movie.

This 1986 gem gave us the infamous "Bueller, Bueller" line, Matthew Broderick rocking out to "Twist and Shout," and so much more. Here's to you and your ingenious scheming, Ferris Bueller! (Bueller.)

Note: *If you're a light drinker, skip rules 1 and 8.*

DRINK OF THE GAME

THE HOOKY HURRICANE

C'mon, Cameron, just one sip.

MAKES 2 DRINKS

4 ounces light rum
4 ounces dark rum
4 ounces passion fruit juice
2 ounces orange juice
Juice of 1 lime
2 tablespoons simple syrup
2 tablespoons grenadine
Orange slices and maraschino cherries, for garnish

Pour all the ingredients except the orange and cherries into a cocktail shaker and shake well. Strain into two chilled hurricane glasses. Top each drink with a maraschino cherry and orange slice.

DRINK WHEN...

1. FERRIS TALKS TO THE CAMERA
2. JEANIE'S JEALOUS
3. **PHONY**
4. → **CALLS**

FERRIS PRESSURES CAMERON

5. BORED STUDENTS
6. FERRIS SINGS -OR- DANCES 7. **"SICK"**

8.

CAMERON'S DAD'S FERRARI

9. BEN STEIN REPEATS A WORD

10. ROONEY PLOTS AGAINST FERRIS

11. CAMERON MENTIONS HIS DAD

12. BEN STEIN STRESSES THE CAR

13. CAMERON OVER THE CAR

14. ROONEY GETS HURT

15. FERRIS IS ALMOST BUSTED

← 16. DOWNTOWN CHICAGO

17. SOMEONE WISHES FERRIS A SPEEDY RECOVERY

TRIVIA

KNOCKOFF
To be friendlier on the wallet, Cameron's dad's Ferrari is a phony made of fiberglass.

SOMEONE NEEDS A NAP!
Charlie Sheen stayed awake for more than 48 hours to achieve that drugged-out look in his scenes with Jeanie at the police station.

ALL IN THE FAMILY
Emilio Estevez—Charlie Sheen's brother—declined the role of Cameron, which went to Alan Ruck, who was 29 at the time.

REAL-LIFE LOVE!
Ferris and Jeanie's parents, played by Cindy Pickett and Lyman Ward, married after the film wrapped. On-screen siblings Matthew Broderick and Jennifer Grey also became engaged after the film. Lucky duck, Grey was also once engaged to Johnny Depp.

NAME GAME
Sloane is named after the daughter of then-Paramount head Ned Tanen. The character's original name was Tandy.

HOT TOPICS

1. *Did you ever catch a sibling in a lie? Did you snitch?*
2. *What was the most epic lie you told to get out of going to school?*
3. *Were you a Ferris, Cameron, or Jeanie in high school?*

ON THE LINE

No one pulls off a prank call quite like Ferris Bueller. He's kind of a legend. Of course, he reigned during the days before caller ID, so you'll need to be a bit more creative. Go around in a circle and have each person prank call a friend. Whoever successfully pulls off the prank using the most outrageous story is Ferris's proud protégé.

FIGHT CLUB

By writing this, we're breaking the first rule of *Fight Club*. And the second rule, for that matter. But what's the fun in keeping something so badass to yourself? It's time to gather your own support group and give this classic the proper drinking-game treatment.

For the uninitiated, *Fight Club* tells the story of The Narrator, played by Edward Norton. The 30-something everyman (hence, the lack of a name) is complacently moving through his life, finding miniscule amounts of joy in his IKEA catalog. He wants change, but doesn't know where to begin. Enter Tyler Durden. And lye burns. And bombings. And acrobatic sex marathons. And much more mayhem.

So celebrate this gloriously anarchic flick without fear of a face pummeling. The only thing hurting will be your liver!

Note: *If you're a light drinker, skip rules 4 and 12.*

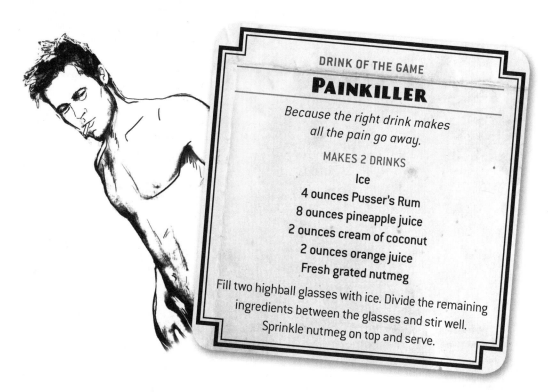

DRINK OF THE GAME

PAINKILLER

*Because the right drink makes
all the pain go away.*

MAKES 2 DRINKS

Ice

4 ounces Pusser's Rum

8 ounces pineapple juice

2 ounces cream of coconut

2 ounces orange juice

Fresh grated nutmeg

Fill two highball glasses with ice. Divide the remaining ingredients between the glasses and stir well. Sprinkle nutmeg on top and serve.

DRINK WHEN...

1. THE RULES ARE MENTIONED
2. "PROJECT MAYHEM"
3. ANYONE SAYS "TYLER DURDEN"
4. ANYONE SMOKES
5. SOAP IS SHOWN OR MENTIONED
6. MARLA SINGER
7. "I AM JACK'S..." VOICEOVER
8.  OR  PRODUCT PLACEMENT

9. ANYONE
FIGHTS

10. ANYONE
BLEEDS

11. CHEMICAL BURN SCARS

12. "FIGHT CLUB"

13. ↘
-QUICK-
-FLASH-
OF
TYLER

14. PENGUIN

15. ANY MENTION OF
ROBERT PAULSON,
BOB, OR
BITCH TITS

16.
TYLER IS SHIRTLESS

TRIVIA

ABORTED DREAMS

Originally, after the marathon sex scene, Marla said, "I want to have your abortion." However, the Fox 2000 Pictures President of Production Laura Ziskin objected. Director David Fincher said he would change it only if the new line couldn't be cut. Ziskin agreed and Fincher rewrote the line to, "I haven't been fucked like that since grade school." When she saw the replacement line, she was even more appalled and requested the original line be kept. But that wasn't the deal she'd signed!

BREAKING THE RULES

Though *Fight Club* is based on a novel, this is the rare exception to the rule that the book is always better than the film. Author Chuck Palahniuk has stated he found the flick to be an improvement to his 1996 novel.

COFFEE ADDICTION

Director David Fincher has said as humans, we're in a society of shoppers when we're designed to be hunters, and his film makes a statement on the amount of consumerism around us. For example, you'll see a white Starbucks coffee cup in most of the film's scenes.

WARNING SIGNS

After the copyright warning on the DVD, another warning flashes on the screen for just one second. Blink and you'll miss Tyler's message.

OH YEAH

For their unseen sex scenes, Brad Pitt and Helena Bonham Carter spent three days recording orgasmic sounds. And for the sex scene that is shown, they posed in ten different Kama Sutra positions.

CHUNKY MONKEY

Meat Loaf's fat suit weighed over 100 pounds. The breasts and love handles were filled with birdseed to give the impression of sagging flesh. Sexy.

HOT TOPICS

1. *Fuck, Marry, Kill: Brad Pitt, Edward Norton, Jared Leto.*

2. *Would you rather have your hand burned by lye or get the shit beat out of you by Bob, aka Bitch Tits?*

3. *What's the worst fight you've ever been in?*

FIGHTING YOURSELF

At the 2000 MTV Movie Awards, Edward Norton was up for the Best Fight Award—for fighting himself. Have you got those acting chops? Take that motivation and give us your best reaction to a fake punch. Draw numbers to decide the order of performances. After everyone's had their turn, you cast your vote to decide the winner. (Don't vote for yourself. That's pathetic.) The person with the most votes wins.

Note: *Place pillows or couch cushions down on the ground to pad the falls of those who are really committed to their stunt work.*

GHOSTBUSTERS

If you've had a dose of a freaky ghost, you better call Ghostbusters! Man, that song is catchy. And it brings us just as much childhood nostalgia as the unforgettable 1984 movie. *Ghostbusters* is one flick that will never lose its cool factor.

Whether it's the amazingly outdated graphics, the sight of a Godzilla-sized marshmallow man ready to attack NYC, or the awesomeness of Bill Murray's one-liners ("We came, we saw, we kicked its ass!"), *Ghostbusters* has it all. Plus, it was way ahead of its time in talking about the end of the world. Here's to the ghost apocalypse!

Note: *If you're a light drinker, skip rules 1 and 17.*

DRINK OF THE GAME

STAY PUFT S'MORETINI

Too many, and you might feel like the floor of a taxi cab.

MAKES 2 DRINKS

4 ounces Smirnoff Fluffed Marshmallow Vodka
4 ounces dark chocolate liqueur
2 ounces cream
Ice
Jet-Puffed jumbo marshmallows

Pour the vodka, dark liqueur, and cream into a cocktail shaker filled with ice. Shake well, and strain into martini glasses. Top each drink with a couple marshmallows.

DRINK WHEN...

1. MENTION OF KEYMASTER OR GATEKEEPER

2.

3. "WHEN SOMEONE ASKS IF YOU ARE A GOD YOU SAY 'YES'!"

4. SOMEONE SAYS "ZUUL"

5. EERIE MUSIC PLAYS

6. Venkman FLIRTS

7. A RECOGNIZABLE COP FROM FAMILY MATTERS

8. GHOSTBUSTERS ALARM SOUNDS

9. 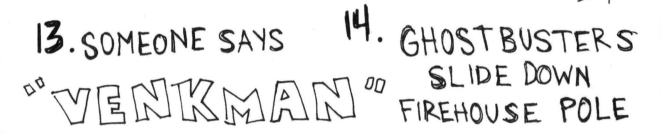 GHOSTBUSTERS COMMERCIAL —AIRS—

10. GHOSTBUSTERS THEME SONG PLAYS

11. "HE SLIMED ME"

12. LOUIS GETS LOCKED OUT

13. SOMEONE SAYS "VENKMAN"

14. GHOSTBUSTERS SLIDE DOWN FIREHOUSE POLE

15. VENKMAN SAYS HE'S A "SCIENTIST"

16.

GHOST TRAP

17. ANY MENTION OF:
- THE END OF THE WORLD
- THE APOCALYPSE
- JUDGMENT DAY

TRIVIA

MARSHMALLOW PREMONITIONS

There are two references to Stay Puft marshmallows in the flick prior to the Stay Puft marshmallow man attacking NYC. The first is a bag of marshmallows on Dana's countertop in the scene where the eggs cook themselves. The second is when the beam of light streams out of the Ghostbusters' firehouse, and a billboard advertises the snack.

CALL ME MAYBE

When the film was still in theaters, director Ivan Reitman had the Ghostbusters' ad air on TV in hopes of increasing the box office gross. He replaced the 555 number with a 1-800 number, which allowed people to call the line. Bill Murray and Dan Aykroyd recorded a message for the phone line, which received up to 1,000 calls per hour, 24 hours a day for six weeks.

WRITER'S BLOCK

It's the hit song that almost didn't happen. Singer and songwriter Ray Parker Jr. was stumped when trying to pen the theme song for the film. He was finally inspired by the Ghostbusters TV commercial to write a song more like an advertising jingle. The song was a number-one hit for weeks.

BELIEVE IT OR NOT

Fans can visit the Ghostbusters headquarters in NYC's TriBeCa neighborhood. Exterior shots were filmed at the Hook and Ladder #8 Firehouse.

HOT TOPICS

1. *Do you believe in ghosts or any other supernatural life forces?*
2. *Have you ever felt the presence of a ghost or thought something was haunted?*

MARSHMALLOW MOUTH

We bring you the marshmallow-mouth challenge, aka Chubby Bunny. Depending on the number of participants, you'll need a bag or two of jumbo marshmallows. Each player will place a marshmallow in their mouth, then say, "Chubby Bunny." If they are able to state the whole phrase coherently, they move along to the next round. Each successful player then adds an additional marshmallow to the one already in his or her mouth and states the phrase again. When a player fails to say the phrase clearly, he or she is eliminated from the game. The cycle continues until one player remains. The winner of the game is the player who fits the most marshmallows into his or her mouth.

THE GOONIES

Goonies never say die! But after a few too many of the drink below, you may beg to differ.

Back in 1985, Sean Astin, Corey Feldman, and Josh Brolin were just kids out to save their homes, find One-Eyed Willy's legendary treasure, and avoid the criminal Fratellis at all costs.

Add in a few more somewhat foul-mouthed goonies and one Sloth, and hey youuuu guyssssss, let's have some fun!

Note: *If you're a light drinker, skip rules 6, 13, and 16.*

DRINK OF THE GAME

GOLDEN TREASURE

Avoid walking near planks after a few of these.

MAKES 4 DRINKS

12 ounces Goldschlager cinnamon schnapps
8 ounces grenadine
28 ounces lemonade
Ice

Pour the Goldschlager, grenadine, and lemonade into a pitcher and stir well. Pour into four glasses filled with ice.

DRINK WHEN...

1. SOMEONE MENTIONS "ONE-EYED" WILLY

2.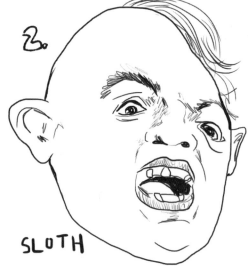

SLOTH

3. DATA USES ONE OF HIS INVENTIONS

4. "HEY, YOU GUYS!"

5. CHUNK EATS

6. SKULL

7.

GOLD & TREASURE

8. MIKEY USES HIS INHALER

9. SOMEONE SHOOTS A GUN

10. SPANISH MAP

11. MOUTH TRANSLATES

12. MIKEY TALKS ABOUT LOSING THEIR HOMES

13. "BOOBY TRAP"

14. THE FRATELLIS ARGUE

15. → A GOONIE SWEARS

16. MA

07. CHUNK IS ACCUSED OF LYING

TRIVIA

OH SHIP
One-Eyed Willy's ship was constructed for the film but kept under wraps. When the kids finally saw it for the first time while filming, some instinctively said, "Holy shit!" and so reshots were needed.

CLOSET RAIDER
John Matuszak, who played Sloth, was a former Oakland Raiders defensive player and wears a shirt with his former team's name in the movie.

BOY OF HIS WORD
In the scene where rocks fall and Data yells, "Holy," and then spells S-H-I-T, it's because Jonathan Ke Quan promised his mom he wouldn't swear in the movie.

ONE MAN'S TRASH...
Sean Astin kept the treasure map, but years later his mom mistook it for just a piece of paper and tossed it. Oopsy.

HOT TOPICS

1. *Share a wish you made in a wishing well.*

2. *If you invented something awesome like Data does, what would it be?*

CANDY BARATHON!

As a nod to Chunk tossing Sloth a Baby Ruth bar, break a few candy bars into a few pieces each. Then pick teams of two—one person's the tosser, one's the catcher—and each team takes a few pieces of the candy bars. Whichever team can continually throw the chocolate and catch it using only their mouths (no hands!) wins, but once the candy hits the floor, you're out.

HAROLD & KUMAR GO TO WHITE CASTLE

After two best friends—with an equal love for pot and White Castle—get a craving for those incomparable tiny burgers (McWhat?), they set off on an epic New Jersey adventure to satisfy their growling stomachs.

But soon after leaving Hoboken, Harold and Kumar discover a Burger Shack has replaced their beloved White Castle. Dun. Dun. Dun. And so, their quest down to White Castle's Cherry Hill location begins, and the duo must evade egomaniac officers, poser skater punks, and yes, one smoked-up cheetah.

Oh, and add Neil Patrick Harris to that list. We always knew Doogie Howser was a badass.

Note: *If you're a light drinker, skip rules 1, 6, 12, and 13.*

DRINK OF THE GAME

CHEETAH MARGARITA

Hold on tight or you'll splat like Harold.

MAKES 2 DRINKS

1 lime, cut into wedges
Superfine sugar
Crushed ice
4 ounces triple sec
12 ounces tequila
12 ounces frozen limeade concentrate

Run a lime wedge around the rim of each margarita glass and roll in superfine sugar. Fill a blender with crushed ice and add the triple sec, tequila, and frozen limeade concentrate. Blend until smooth and serve in the sugared margarita glasses. Garnish each drink with a lime slice.

DRINK WHEN...

1. MARIJUANA

HAROLD & KUMAR
DO SOMETHING

2. ILLEGAL

3.

MARIA

4. KUMAR PISSES OFF HAROLD

5. HAROLD AND KUMAR ENTER A **NEW** NEW JERSEY TOWN

6. "BURGER"

7. KUMAR LIES

8. YOU **FEEL HUNGRY** WATCHING THIS MOVIE

9. **COP**

10. CHEETAH MENTION OR SIGHTING

11. SOMEONE STEALS A CAR

12. "EXTREME"

white Castle

13.

15. NPH!

14. **HAROLD** TALKS ABOUT **HIS WORK**

16. GOLDSTEIN AND ROSENBERG GET HIGH OR EAT HOT DOGS

HOT TOPICS

1. Which fast food chain has the best burgers?

2. What's the worst thing your roommate has done to you? Or to your car?

TRIVIA

HAM IT UP
Rosenberg and Goldstein are named after the characters Rosencrantz and Guildenstern in Shakespeare's *Hamlet*.

NPH 4EVA
Rumor has it that Neil Patrick Harris landed the role of womanizer Barney Stinson on *How I Met Your Mother* after the sitcom's casting powers saw (and loved) his parody of himself in this film.

SLIDER CHALLENGE!

Everyone throws down money and you order a ton of sliders from your favorite joint. It's pretty simple: Whoever eats the most without puking is the burger, err, king.

THE HANGOVER

What happens in Vegas...becomes a smashing box office success and turns into a trilogy.

The Hangover gifted Zach Galifianakis with his breakout role, and the world hasn't looked back since. After surviving the wrath of Tyson...and roofies...and an angry, naked Asian man, the fellas take their bachelor debauchery to Thailand in the sequel.

But before we get ahead of ourselves, let's agree to play the game below and then never speak of it again.

Note: *If you're a light drinker, skip rules 1, 2, and 8.*

DRINK OF THE GAME

VEGAS STRIPPER SPRITZER

Inspired by Carlos, err, Tyler's mama. No roofies, Alan!

MAKES 2 DRINKS

Ice

9 ounces chilled red or white wine

4 ounces club soda

Orange wedges, for garnish

Fill two wine glasses with ice and top each with the wine and club soda. Stir and garnish with an orange wedge.

DRINK WHEN...

1. ALAN SAYS SOMETHING RIDICULOUS

2. SOMEONE GETS HURT

3. MR. CHOW LAUGHS

4.  TIGER

5. SATCHEL

6. GAMBLING

7. MELISSA SLEPT WITH a BARTENDER. or SAILOR. or BELLHOP.

8. ANYONE SAYS "VEGAS"

WELCOME TO Fabulous LAS VEGAS NEVADA

9. STU CALLS HIMSELF A DOCTOR

10. ALAN TALKS ABOUT THEIR *friendship*

11. BABY CARLOS

12. "DON'T REMEMBER"

13. SOMEONE TALKS ABOUT A WEDDING

14.

MIKE TYSON

15. WARNING: DON"T MESS UP THE CAR

16. THE GUYS SEE SOMEONE FROM THE NIGHT BEFORE

17. SOMEONE MENTIONS FINDING DOUG

TRIVIA

CHEW ON THAT

Stu's missing tooth? That's real! Ed Helms never had an adult incisor, so he simply popped out his fake one for filming.

RAWWRRR

Mike Tyson really owns a tiger. Make that seven tigers.

SPEAKING OF SEVEN...

Three sets of twin babies (and a dummy!) were used to film Tyler's too cool part.

BIG BUSTS

Paul Rudd turned down playing Phil, and Jack Black declined the role of Alan. Lindsay Lohan was offered Heather Graham's part, but she too passed, thinking the movie would be a box office bomb. Yeah, about that, LiLo...

HOT TOPICS

1. What's the most valuable thing you ever stole or wrecked?
2. Would you have your bachelor or bachelorette party in Vegas?

STEAL MIKE TYSON'S TIGER

Just kidding. Although Alan would be so proud! Ed Helms and Zach Galifianakis improvised "Stu's Song" and "Three Best Friends," so now it's your turn. Go around the room with each person adding a line to the song. If you hesitate and break the flow, you're out. Last person singing is the night's idol. Oh, and don't forget to record this.

HOME ALONE

Sure, *It's A Wonderful Life* has angels getting their wings. And Tim Allen can slide down nonexistent chimneys in *The Santa Clause*. But in *Home Alone*, Kevin McCallister has the ultimate power: He can make his family disappear.

So, what's an unsupervised eight-year-old to do? Order pizza, watch a mob movie, and save his home from dimwitted robbers—with potty mouths. Director Chris Columbus recommended to Joe Pesci that he switch his accidental F-bombs during the filming of Harry's flip-out scenes to "fridge." And listen closely—IMDB says Daniel Stern slips and says "shit" while grabbing his boot through the doggy door.

While those are true-to-life reactions, let's toast this classic Christmas film…that probably wouldn't have made much sense if cell phones were around in 1990.

Note: *If you're a light drinker, skip rules 7, 13, and 15.*

DRINK OF THE GAME

THE WET BANDIT

You guys give up, or are you thirsty for more?

MAKES 2 DRINKS

Ice
4 ounces coconut rum
Pineapple juice
1 ounce blue curaçao
Maraschino cherries, for garnish

Fill two hurricane glasses with ice and divide the rum between them. Fill with pineapple juice, leaving room at the top for the blue curaçao. Add ½ ounce curaçao to each glass, stir, and top each with a maraschino cherry.

DRINK WHEN...

1. A FAMILY MEMBER RAGS ON KEVIN

2. KEVIN'S **SCARED**

3. UNCLE FRANK ACTS LIKE AN **ASS**

4. KEVIN SCREAMS

5. KEVIN GOES INTO BUZZ'S ROOM

6. "**HOME ALONE**"

7. KEVIN **FOOLS** SOMEBODY

8. **THE GOLD TOOTH**

9. HARRY AND MARV ARGUE

10. KEVIN MISSES HIS FAMILY

11. CHRISTMAS MUSIC PLAYS

12.
OLD MAN MARLEY

13. ANYONE MENTIONS SANTA OR X-MAS

14. GUS POLINSKI

15. HARRY OR MARV GETS INJURED

16. PARIS

17. MRS. MCCALLISTER'S ON AN AIRPORT

18. TARANTULA

TRIVIA

OUCH, DUDE!

When Harry attempts to bite Kevin's finger, Joe Pesci actually did bite Macaulay Culkin and even left a scar on his finger. Poor kid!

SCARED OF SPIDERS, MARV?

Daniel Stern would only let Buzz's tarantula be placed on his face for one take. His scream was faked and the infamous yell was added later.

QUICK THINKING

Kevin's "You guys give up, or are you thirsty for more?" one-liner was improvised, as was John Candy's tale about leaving his kid at a funeral home.

HOT TOPICS

1. Would you rather scorch your head, burn your hand on a heated doorknob, or step on a nail?

2. Marv and Harry were the Wet Bandits; what would your robbery ring name be?

SAY AHHHHH!

Put your hands on your cheeks and scream! The yell closest to Kevin McCallister's post-shower scream wins.

THE KARATE KID

The 1984 flick is the ultimate story of an underdog coming out on top. And (spoiler alert!) get this—*The Karate Kid* screenwriter Dennis Palumbo wanted to rewrite the ending so that Daniel lost the last fight. (He said, "You can't have Mr. Miyagi tell him, 'It doesn't matter if you win or lose,' for 90 minutes and then have to have him win.") Can you imagine if Daniel-san couldn't take down his bully and lost the girl? No thanks. Snoozefest.

The Karate Kid is unlike most high school dramedies. It has more heart and really focuses on the relationship between Daniel and the wise Mr. Miyagi, who always had advice for his teenage buddy. Our favorite? "Man who catch fly with chopstick accomplish anything." And we can't forget to thank Miyagi for giving us "Wax on, wax off," a movie quote that will live on forever.

Note: *If you're a light drinker, skip rules 1, 5, and 14.*

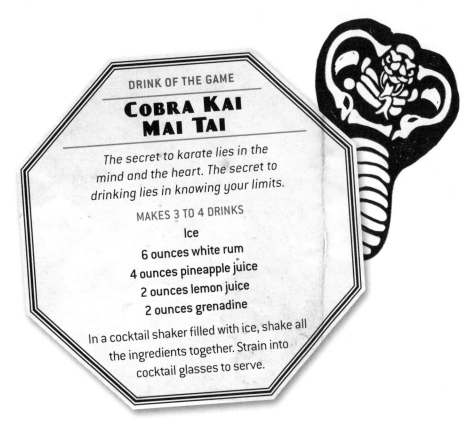

DRINK OF THE GAME

COBRA KAI MAI TAI

The secret to karate lies in the mind and the heart. The secret to drinking lies in knowing your limits.

MAKES 3 TO 4 DRINKS

Ice
6 ounces white rum
4 ounces pineapple juice
2 ounces lemon juice
2 ounces grenadine

In a cocktail shaker filled with ice, shake all the ingredients together. Strain into cocktail glasses to serve.

DRINK WHEN...

1. ANYONE SAYS "MIYAGI"

2. DANIEL FLIRTS WITH ALI →

3. "KARATE"

4. ANYONE TALKS ABOUT COBRA KAI CODE: STRIKE FIRST STRIKE HARD NO MERCY

5. ANYONE BOWS

6. SOMEONE GETS INJURED

7. "WAX ON, WAX OFF."

8. COBRAS SAY, "SENSEI"

9. SYNTHESIZER MUSIC PLAYS

10. DANIEL TRAINS

11. COBRA KAI LOGO

12. DANIEL GETS BEAT UP

13. MIYAGI DROPS SOME WISDOM

14. "DANIEL-SAN"

15. "YOU'RE PRETTY OK, TOO."

TRIVIA

BABY FACE
Believe it or not, during filming in 1983, star Ralph Macchio was actually 22 years old. Many of his cast-mates were stunned when they asked his age.

DREAM CAR
The yellow classic car that Daniel waxes and then receives as a birthday gift from Mr. Miyagi was given to Ralph by a producer. He still owns it today.

CHEATERS NEVER PROSPER
The fly in the chopstick scene is attached to a fishing line. A crew member controlled where it would go. Oh, movie magic!

HOT TOPICS
1. Who is your arch nemesis?
2. What's the meanest thing you've ever done to get back at somebody?

CRANE KICK CONTEST
Who can do the most crane kicks in a row? For the safety of you and your friends, pile as many pillows as possible in the area behind where each person will kick. In case anyone falls, they'll have a soft landing.

LEGALLY BLONDE

We love movies that remind you that you can accomplish anything when you set your mind to it.

Elle Wood's inspiring story of going from heartbroken sorority girl to Harvard Law School graduate is one we never tire of seeing. Seriously, if *Legally Blonde* is on TBS, we will plop on our couch for two hours to see Elle "bend and snap," rise to the top, and leave loser Warner in her dust.

Similar to *Clueless*'s Cher, Elle isn't just a dumb blonde. She's full of wisdom. We agree—whoever did say orange was the new pink is seriously disturbed. Getting an awesome internship can be so much better than spending four amazing hours in the hot tub with your boyfriend after winter formal. And it is impossible to use a half-loop stitching on low-viscosity rayon.

So here's to Elle and Bruiser, our two favorite Gemini vegetarians, proving everyone wrong!

Note: *If you're a light drinker, skip rules 9 and 11.*

DRINK OF THE GAME

PLATINUM BLONDE

Drinkable no matter what color your hair is.

MAKES 2 DRINKS

4 ounces white rum

1 ounce cream

1 ounce orange liqueur

Ice

Combine the ingredients over ice in a cocktail shaker. Shake well.

Strain into two cocktail glasses.

DRINK WHEN....

1. **COSMOPOLITAN**

2.

3. **BEND & SNAP**

4. REFERENCES TO **BEING BLONDE**

5. ELLE IS AT A SALON

6. VIVIAN IS RUDE TO ELLE

7. **LEGAL JARGON**

8. ELLE NAME-DROPS A CELEB

9. ELLE HAS A NEW HAIRSTYLE

10. ANY REFERENCE TO ELLE
BECOMING SERIOUS

11. ELLE WEARS PINK ♥

12.

UPS GUY

13. SORORITY SQUEALS

14. ΔΝ
DELTA NU

"POOH

15. BEAR"

16. PAULETTE IS SPEECHLESS
— OR MUMBLES

TRIVIA

SORORITY STEREOTYPES

To research her role as Elle, Reese Witherspoon spent two weeks analyzing the behavior of sorority girls. She didn't want to portray Elle as a stereotype. On the DVD commentary, Reese said the sorority girls she met were all very kind and she enjoyed her time with them. She also studied women shopping at Neiman Marcus, and attended law school classes for a day.

TOP OF THE CLASS

A perfect score on the LSAT exam is 180. Elle's score of 179 would put her in the 0.1 percentile.

HAIR CARE

The film's producers intentionally styled Elle's hair differently for every scene. In total? That's about 40 looks for our favorite law student!

THEY KNOW THEY CAN DANCE

Now-famous dance choreographers (and adorable couple) Napoleon and Tabitha D'Umo (aka Nappytabs) are the brains behind the "Bend and Snap" routine. They are now regular choreographers for the hit Fox show *So You Think You Can Dance*?

BEND & SNAP BATTLES

Oh my god, the bend and snap! Works every time! Determine who among you and your friends has the best bend and snap. Like any tournament, two participants will face off at a time. The rest of the group will act as judges to determine who has the better bend and snap, and will move on to the next round. Continue the battles until one person is deemed the winner. Remember, it's really all about the snap pose—the bigger, the better!

MAGIC MIKE

Ladies who are reading this! We had to do you at least one solid by putting such a man-candy movie on this list. You can thank us later when the sexy Channing Tatum comes onto your TV screen showing off his spectacular abs while grinding on stage. We don't blame you if you're hootin' and hollerin' and trying to throw dollar bills at the screen.

As we all know, *Magic Mike* is loosely based on Tatum's own experiences as a stripper. And damn, do we wish we had been a recipient of a Chan-Chan lap dance! But the movie isn't all just dance music, ripped men, banana hammocks, waxed chests, and sexy moves. Director Steven Soderbergh takes the movie to a dark place, where the cash flows heavy and the drugs run rampant. Friendships are betrayed and lifelong dreams just might not come true. But, let's be honest, we really only care about the hotties, their bodies, and Big Dick Richie.

Note: *If you're a light drinker, skip rules 1 and 3.*

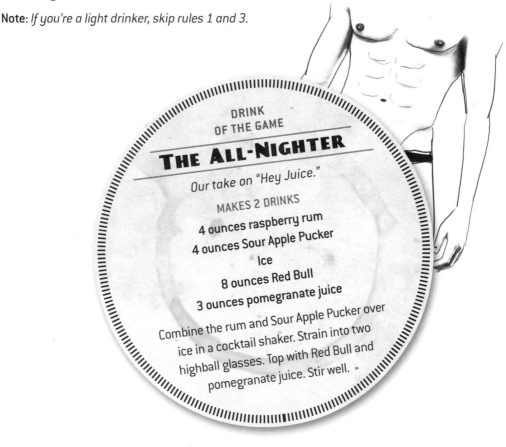

DRINK
OF THE GAME

THE ALL-NIGHTER

Our take on "Hey Juice."

MAKES 2 DRINKS

4 ounces raspberry rum

4 ounces Sour Apple Pucker

Ice

8 ounces Red Bull

3 ounces pomegranate juice

Combine the rum and Sour Apple Pucker over ice in a cocktail shaker. Strain into two highball glasses. Top with Red Bull and pomegranate juice. Stir well.

DRINK WHEN...

→ 1. ANYONE GYRATES

2. ANY MENTION OF LIFE DREAMS

3. BEAUTIFUL WASHBOARD ABS →

4. BIG DICK RICHIE NAME - DROP

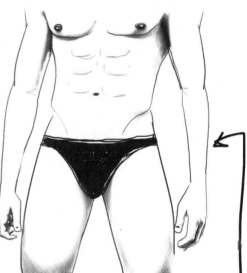

5. MAN THONGS

6. TEACUP PIG

7. BROMANCE AND MENTORING

8. CLOTHING IS REMOVED

9. MASCULINE VIOLENCE

"ALL RIGHT
ALL RIGHT
ALL RIGHT"

10.

11. DRUG USE

12. CROTCH GRAB

13. STRIPPING MONTAGE

14. ASS-LESS CHAPS

15. STEREOTYPICAL STRIPPER COSTUME

16. STRIPPING SOLO

TRIVIA

FULL MONTY

Matthew McConaughey almost went full-frontal during his stripping scene! At one point, he has to roll away from all the women in the audience because they're getting way too handsy—they accidentally ripped his G-string! Like a professional, he doesn't stop his dance or end the scene. You can even see him grabbing his junk as to not let "Krull the Warrior King" make an appearance.

WORKIN' HARD FOR THE MONEY

No stunt butts were harmed in the making of this movie. In fact, the *Magic Mike* stars were more than ready to show off their hard-earned muscles. "There wasn't one stunt butt or stunt dancers for any of the dances," Channing Tatum said. "No way—that's all me up there, I don't need a stunt ass," adds McConaughey. And you certainly won't hear us complaining. These guys' bodies are REAL—and they're spectacular!

(ALMOST) NO FOR JOE

The sexy Joe Manganiello hesitated on accepting the role of Big Dick Richie because of how much time he already spends shirtless on HBO's *True Blood*. Fortunately for us, comedian Chris Rock gave Joe some sound advice and encouraged him to take the role: "Chris was the one who talked me into doing *Magic Mike*" Joe recalls. "Chris said, motherf*cker, they're gonna hate you anyway. You might as well work with Steven Soderberg."

HOT TOPICS

1. *Fuck, Marry, Kill: Channing Tatum, Joe Manganiello, Matthew McConaughey*

2. *Would you rather be a stripper for the rest of your life or be married to a stripper for the rest of your life?*

AMATEUR NIGHT

It's your turn to take the stage! Put on some classic stripper music (like Def Leppard's "Pour Some Sugar on Me" or Ginuwine's "Pony") and show us what you've got. Each person gets 45 seconds to show off their best moves while the "audience" scores the dirty performance on a scale of 1 to 10, 1 being tame and 10 being downright dirrrrty. The person with the highest score wins. This works best when there's a mix of guys and gals!

MEAN GIRLS

Girl World is a treacherous place, so consider yourself warned. Add a high school cafeteria to the mix and you're talking about a domain more dangerous than the African jungle. Rawwwr.

Mean Girls, written by self-proclaimed "supernerd" Tina Fey (we love you, T!), shows how one misstep in Girl World means getting nearly pancaked by a bus. For the queen bees, aka the "Plastics," there are rules to be obeyed—like on Wednesdays, they wear pink. Should you break these feminine bylaws, you will have started social warfare and can kiss eating lunch with the fierce ones buh-bye.

Considered an instant teen cult success when it was released in 2004, *Mean Girls* resonated with the masses because of the harsh cattiness that stings incredibly true to the real world. So what better way to help you forget all the dramz of your high school years than to drown your frenemy sorrows? Step 1: Make a batch of jungle juice. Step 2: Read the drinking game rules. Step 3: Discover who among your friends survived the worst gossip. Sure, we believe you when you say none of it was true.

Note: *If you're a light drinker, skip rule 2, 6, and 9.*

DRINK OF THE GAME

JUNGLE JUICE

Sip while wearing a pink shirt to be extra fetch.

MAKES 30 TO 40 DRINKS

1 (1.75-liter) bottle dark rum
2 (1.75-liter) bottles light rum
1 gallon (16 cups) orange juice
1 gallon (16 cups) pineapple juice
8 cups sweet and sour mix
1 (12-ounce) bottle grenadine
Large bag of ice
3 oranges, sliced
3 apples, sliced
1 pineapple, peeled and sliced

Mix all the liquids together in a large container and add the ice. Add sliced oranges, apples, and pineapple.

DRINK WHEN...

1.

2. CADY'S VOICEOVER

3. 3-WAY PHONE CALLS

4. HIGH SCHOOL / AFRICAN JUNGLE COMPARISONS

5. → KALTEEN BAR

6. AARON SAMUELS

7. MS. NORBURY WHINES

8. SOMEONE MISPRONOUNCES CADY'S NAME

9. SNL - ALUM SIGHTING

10. GRETCHEN DROPS A REGINA BOMB

11. ⬅ SPEEDING SCHOOL BUS

12.
MATHLETES

13. "I WANT MY PINK SHIRT BACK!"

14. JANIS HATES ON REGINA

15. "YOU CAN'T SIT WITH US!"

16. "FETCH"

17. CADY EATS LUNCH IN A BATHROOM STALL

TRIVIA

BITCHY MOVE

Lindsay Lohan was originally cast as Regina George. But she became worried about her image and being labeled a "bitch," so she took the role of Cady instead. One producer is rumored as saying Rachel McAdams was cast at the queen bee because "only nice girls can play mean girls." Put that in the Burn Book!

DOWN A NOTCH

In a cafeteria scene where Cady was asked if her "muffin was buttered," the line was originally written as, "Is your cherry popped?" Dirty! It was taken out to help bring the MPAA rating down from R to PG-13.

HOT TOPICS

1. *What's the worst rumor you ever heard in high school? Was it true?*

2. *What were you voted in high school? What should you have been voted?*

TRUST ME!

You know the drill: Line up your buds and—go ahead—fess something you've been dying to get off your chest. Yes, you did borrow your friend's car without asking and yes, you did peep at your roommate's text inbox. Twice. But one suggestion, how about falling into the couch or a stack of fluffy pillows instead of, you know, your tipsy amigos' extended arms? Otherwise we foresee an epic Gretchen Wieners splat.

MONTY PYTHON & THE HOLY GRAIL

It's a busy life in Camelot.

Often considered one of the greatest comedies ever made, *Monty Python & the Holy Grail* has been ranked as an all-time favorite for nearly four decades. The 1975 film was the first full-length feature to be composed of new material from the Monty Python comedians.

With wacky, off-topic dialogue, a very, very low budget, and just a few actors playing multiple roles, *Monty Python & the Holy Grail* is a trifecta of comedic genius. The bizarre spoof of King Arthur and his knights on the quest to find the Holy Grail has given us so much to be thankful for. Let's cheers to men in tights, detailed Swallow debates, insults from the French ("Your mother was a hamster and your father smelt of elderberries"), killer rabbits, the Knights who say Ni, and so much more.

Note: *If you're a light drinker, skip rules 1, 5, and 8.*

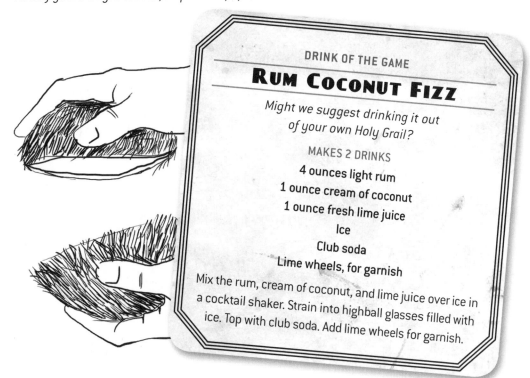

DRINK OF THE GAME

RUM COCONUT FIZZ

Might we suggest drinking it out of your own Holy Grail?

MAKES 2 DRINKS

4 ounces light rum
1 ounce cream of coconut
1 ounce fresh lime juice
Ice
Club soda
Lime wheels, for garnish

Mix the rum, cream of coconut, and lime juice over ice in a cocktail shaker. Strain into highball glasses filled with ice. Top with club soda. Add lime wheels for garnish.

DRINK WHEN...

1. THE HOLY GRAIL IS SHOWN OR MENTIONED

2. THE KNIGHTS RIDE IMAGINARY HORSES

3. ARGUMENTS GO OFF TOPIC

4. STORYBOOK NARRATION

5. "NI"

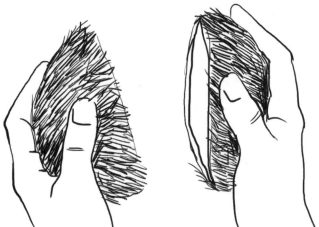

6. ANYONE CLICKS COCONUTS

7. MONKS ARE HEARD CHANTING

8. "SWALLOW"

9.

BLACK KNIGHT
LOSES A LIMB
←

10. "CAMELOT"

11. "BRING OUT YOUR DEAD"

12. "NOT QUITE DEAD"

13. THE KING IS IGNORED

14. BRITISH POLICE

15. SIR BEDEVERE LIFTS THE VISOR ON HIS HELMET

TRIVIA

SWALLOW SCIENCE

The airspeed velocity of an unladen swallow is approximately 24 miles per hour, beating its wings 7 to 9 times per second rather than 43. While it's true a 5-ounce bird cannot carry a 1-pound coconut, no swallow weighs 5 ounces. A barn swallow, which is a species found in Europe, weighs only 20 grams, or two-thirds of an ounce.

UP FOR AUCTION

In March 2007, the helmet worn by Sir Bedevere was featured in an auction of movie costumes. It sold for $29,000, more than ten times the original estimate.

NO BUDGET

The use of coconut shells as a replacement for the sound of galloping horses came about because the production just couldn't afford real horses.

HOT TOPICS

1. What would your name be if you were bestowed the honor of being a Knight of the Round Table?

2. Monty Python & the Holy Grail is considered one of the best comedies of all time. What other movies would you add to that list?

GALLOPING RACE

Since we can't afford real horses either, you're going to have to gallop. Bonus points if you have coconuts to clomp. Remember: Galloping is different than skipping. Here, you keep the same leg in front instead of switching between your legs. For this challenge, decide the distance of your race and make sure everyone knows the path. You must gallop the entire way. The person to gallop and reach the finish line first wins. On your marks. Get set. Go!

NAPOLEON DYNAMITE

Admit it, you would have voted for Pedro.

In this unexpected hit, Napoleon struggles to find his place both at home and school. Gosh. But then his new best friend Pedro, crush Deb, and some sick dance moves turn it all around.

While there's been buzz over the years about a sequel—Pedro goes from rural Idaho to the White House? Kip and Lafawnduh have a football team of kids? Uncle Rico goes pro?—director Jared Hess declines any such fun. Insert deep sigh.

Oh well. Kip, bring me my Chapstick!

Note: *If you're a light drinker, skip rule 7.*

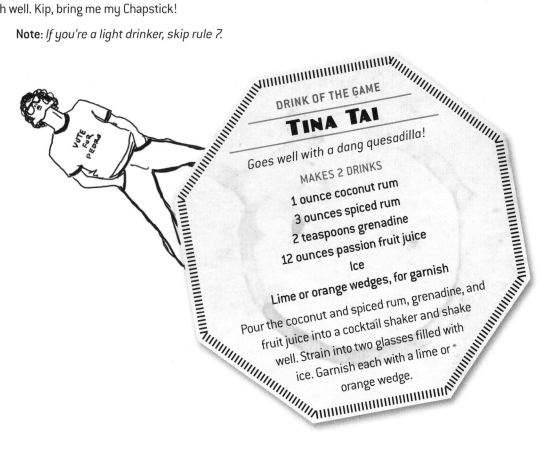

DRINK OF THE GAME

TINA TAI

Goes well with a dang quesadilla!

MAKES 2 DRINKS

1 ounce coconut rum
3 ounces spiced rum
2 teaspoons grenadine
12 ounces passion fruit juice
Ice
Lime or orange wedges, for garnish

Pour the coconut and spiced rum, grenadine, and fruit juice into a cocktail shaker and shake well. Strain into two glasses filled with ice. Garnish each with a lime or orange wedge.

DRINK WHEN...

1. NAPOLEON SIGHS DEEPLY IN DISGUST

2. SOMEONE DOES SIGN LANGUAGE

3. GLAMOUR SHOTS

4. A HIGH SCHOOL STUDENT LOOKS AT LEAST 35

5.  TINA

6. VOTE FOR PEDRO

7. TRAPPER KEEPER -OR- CABOODLE SIGHTING

8. NAPOLEON & KIP WRESTLE

9. UNCLE RICO GETS NOSTALGIC

10. TOTS

11. NAPOLEON BUSTS OUT HIS MOVES

12. CHEESY MUSIC PLAYS

13. "HECK YES!"

14. Lafuwunduh

15. SOMEONE GETS SHOVED INTO A LOCKER

16. SOMEONE DOODLES

TRIVIA

SHE'S A DOLL
Tina's real name isn't Tina. It's Dolly and she belongs to director Jared Hess's mother.

REAL-LIFE LAFAWNDUH
Aaron Ruell's (Kip) wife makes a cameo at the movie's end—she's the woman who rides her bike to see Uncle Rico.

UNDERPAID MUCH?
Jon Heder received $1,000 for his turn as Napoleon Dynamite, and the movie went on to gross more than $40,000,000. Hope he got a bonus!

SEEING DOUBLE. HECK YES.
Jon Heder, who was 27 while playing a high school kid, has an identical twin.

NO STEAK FOR YOU
Uncle Rico's a vegetarian in real life. So all those scenes showing him eating steak? When he wipes his mouth, he's really spitting food into the napkin.

HOT TOPICS

1. *How many times would it take you to throw a pigskin a quarter mile?*
2. *Tater tots or French fries?*

LET'S GET SKETCHY

Everyone draws his or her best liger in honor of Napoleon's favorite animal. Best one becomes everyone's Facebook photo for a week!

OFFICE SPACE

This movie is for anyone and everyone who's ever had a "case of the Mondays."

Been there? Thought so. Although *Office Space* wasn't considered box office gold by any means, it continues to resonate with fed-up employees everywhere who share a deep desire to smash faulty office equipment. Long past the film's 1999 release, it continues to build its cult following—a testament to how few people actually enjoy their jobs?

Screw the 9 to 5—you're not there now. (We hope.) It's time to party and appreciate a guy who really, really loves his stapler and another guy with enough you-know-whats to take the boss's parking spot.

Note: *If you're a light drinker, skip rules 1, 3, 7, and 9.*

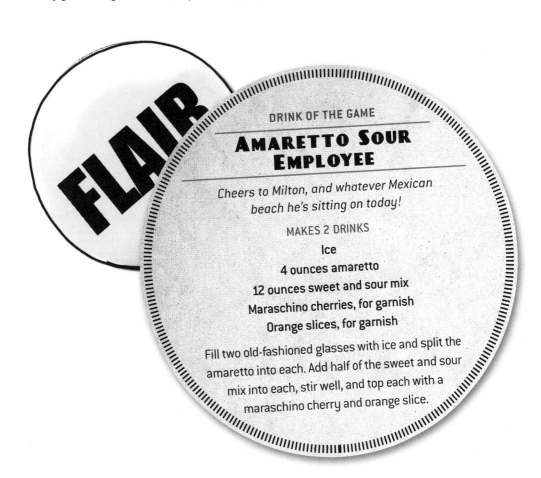

FLAIR

DRINK OF THE GAME

AMARETTO SOUR EMPLOYEE

Cheers to Milton, and whatever Mexican beach he's sitting on today!

MAKES 2 DRINKS

Ice

4 ounces amaretto

12 ounces sweet and sour mix

Maraschino cherries, for garnish

Orange slices, for garnish

Fill two old-fashioned glasses with ice and split the amaretto into each. Add half of the sweet and sour mix into each, stir well, and top each with a maraschino cherry and orange slice.

DRINK WHEN...

1.
INITECH
NAME DROP

2. MILTON MUMBLES

3. LUMBERGH SAYS
"YEAAAH"
"M'KAY"
"WHAT'S -OR-
HAPPENING"

4. SOMEONE MISPRONOUNCES
SAMIR'S LAST NAME

6. 5. RAP MUSIC PLAYS ♫

MICHAEL BOLTON

7. **FLAIR**

8. THE PRINTER FAILS

9. SOMEONE ROCKS SUSPENDERS

10. THE BOBS

11. SAMIR IS SECONDS AWAY FROM A MELTDOWN

12. PETER DOES SOMETHING WRONG AT WORK

13. CASE OF THE MONDAYS

14. SOMEONE BRINGS UP THE → TPS REPORTS

15. LAWRENCE & PETER TALK THROUGH A WALL

16.

TRIVIA

CALLING NAMES

Jennifer Aniston's middle name is Joanna, her character's moniker in the film.

IT'S MY, MY, MY ROLE

Howard Stern's former sidekick Artie Lange auditioned to play Milton.

SORRY, WE'RE CLOSED

The Alligator Grill restaurant in Austin, Texas was used to film Chotchkie's and—despite its movie glory—has shut down.

HOT TOPICS

1. What's the best '90s rap song? (The Fresh Prince of Bel-Air theme song totally counts.)

2. If you could steal $305,326.13, would you? What would you spend it on?

THERAPY

Try to hypnotize anyone in the room. If it works, you win $305,326.13. Just kidding. But everyone should take a shot in your honor.

THE PRINCESS BRIDE

The Princess Bride is a classic fairy tale about true love, sword fights, evil pirates, revenge, kidnappings, torture, and yes, some kissing—and even dudes like it! Just ask Fred Savage.

The 1987 movie has fans both young and old—many of whom first watched it while home sick from school (you, too?!). Everything about the movie is captivating for a young kid. Just as Grandpa says, *The Princess Bride* has everything. We're talking adventure, action, fear, humor, romance...what more could you need in a flick?

Whether you're laughing, crying, biting your nails, or cheering for the characters, *The Princess Bride* has a place in our hearts, which gives it a place in this book. Whenever you feel nostalgic for the days when you had not a care in the world, pop in this classic and get a little tipsy. As you wish, your cares will disappear momentarily while you root for Westley and Princess Buttercup to live happily ever after.

Note: *If you're a light drinker, skip rule 17.*

DRINK OF THE GAME

TRUE LOVE COCKTAIL

This drink is the greatest thing in the world, except for a nice MLT—mutton, lettuce, and tomato sandwich, where the mutton is nice and lean and the tomato is ripe.

MAKES 2 DRINKS

3 ounces coconut rum
2 ounces peach schnapps
2 ounces cranberry juice
Ice
Fresh strawberries, for garnish

Pour the rum, schnapps, and juice over ice in a cocktail shaker. Shake well. Strain into martini glasses and garnish each with a strawberry.

DRINK WHEN...

1. "FARMBOY"

2.  AS YOU WISH

3. MAWWIAGE

4. ANYONE MENTIONS **ANDRE THE GIANT'S** SIZE

5. INCONCEIVABLE!

6. "MY NAME IS INIGO MONTOYA. YOU **KILLED** MY FATHER. PREPARE TO **DIE**."

7.  TRUE LOVE

8. THE GRANDSON —INTERRUPTS—

9. SWORD FIGHT

THE
10. **MACHINE**

11. HORSE RIDES

12. DREAD PIRATE ROBERTS

13. R.O.U.S.

RODENTS OF UNUSUAL SIZE

14. MAN IN **BLACK**

15. WESTLEY DEFEATS A FOE

16. **6**-fingered Man

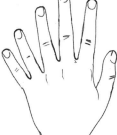

17. PRINCE HUMPERDINCK

18. BUTTERCUP IS REFERRED TO AS
~ HIGHNESS -or- PRINCESS ~

TRIVIA

GIGGLES MCGEE

Director Rob Reiner had to step off set when filming Billy Crystal's scenes because he couldn't contain his laughter. Some say he would be laughing so hard, he'd begin to feel nauseous.

ACHY BREAKY BACK

Life isn't always easier when you're bigger than everyone else. Despite the plotline of Fezzik having nearly Superman-like strength, Andre the Giant's severe back problems prevented him from lifting anything of substantial weight. In the scene where Buttercup jumps from the castle window down to Fezzik and the horses, actress Robin Wright needed to be attached to wires because Andre wouldn't have been able to support her himself.

EXCUSES, EXCUSES

Unsurprisingly, the R.O.U.S. are actually actors inside of rat suits. However, on the day they were to film the scene where Westley battles the giant rats, the "rat actor" was ticketed for speeding and subsequently arrested. The filmmakers had to bail him out of jail so that the scene could be filmed on time.

TOY SWORD FIGHT

First, you will need to purchase two cheap toy swords. Or steal them from little kids. Your life, your choices. Players will form two teams. Each team will take turns as one player challenges a member of the opposing team to a sword fight. To win a sword fight, you must fake stab your enemy three times. The team with the most remaining warriors will be deemed the winners. En garde!

PULP FICTION

You know what they call a Quarter Pounder with Cheese in France? A Royale with Cheese.

Pulp Fiction is truly a pop culture phenomenon. Just think of all the iconic scenes and quotes that have invaded the ether over time. The adrenaline shot to Mia's heart when she overdoses. The Twist dance contest scene starring Vincent and Mia (who doesn't love John Travolta's moves?!). The image of John Travolta and Samuel L. Jackson's characters dressed in suits and ties pointing their guns. "I'ma get medieval on your ass."

Oh, and it's also considered, like, one of the best movies of all time. But meh, not like that's anything to brag about, Tarantino.

Note: *If you're a light drinker, skip rules 1, 5, and 14.*

DRINK OF THE GAME

LIQUID COCAINE

This is some serious gourmet shit.

MAKES 4 DRINKS

2 ounces triple sec
2 ounces amaretto almond liqueur
2 ounces Southern Comfort peach liqueur
2 ounces peach schnapps
12 ounces pineapple juice
12 ounces cranberry juice
4 splashes lemon-lime soda
Maraschino cherries, for garnish

Mix the alcohol in a pitcher. Add the juice. Pour into highball glasses and splash with the soda. Garnish with cherries. Serve.

DRINK WHEN...

1. JULES SAYS "MOTHERFUCKER"

2.
BRIEFCASE LOCK

3. Ezekiel 25:17

4. QUENTIN TARANTINO CAMEO

5. GUNS ARE FIRED

6. ANY DRUGS ARE TAKEN

7.

8.
MIA DANCES

9. BUTCH PULLS A SWORD

10. FOX FORCE FIVE

11. SOMEONE DIES

12. HONEY BUNNY

13.
ROYALE WITH CHEESE

14. F-BOMBS ↓ ARE DROPPED

15. TIRES SQUEAL

16. BUTCH CALLS FABIENNE

Lemon Pie

VINCENT SMOKES

18. WATCH

17.

19. AMSTERDAM

TRIVIA

WHO'S COUNTING?

The word "fuck" is used 265 times. The movie's body count is eight (six on-screen, two mentioned).

CASTING CALL

Quentin Tarantino was indecisive as to which character he would portray: Jimmie or Lance. He decided on Jimmie because he wanted to be behind the camera during Mia's overdose scene.

TO AFRO OR NOT TO AFRO

In the script, Jules's character was supposed to have a gigantic afro. A crewmember brought a variety of afro wigs and one jheri curl to the set. Quentin Tarantino hadn't thought about a jheri curl wig, but Samuel L. Jackson tried it on and Tarantino liked it.

REWIND

The shot of Vincent reviving Mia by plunging the syringe into her chest was filmed by having John Travolta pull it out. Then, in postproduction, the scene was played backward.

THE MILLION DOLLAR QUESTION

According to the script's cowriter, Roger Avary, the original plan was to have the briefcase hold diamonds. The idea seemed rather lackluster, so Avary and Tarantino decided to never show the briefcase's contents. This would allow each viewer to use his or her imagination to decide what best fits the description "so beautiful." In a radio interview with Howard Stern in 2003, Tarantino said, "It's whatever the viewer wants it to be."

HOT TOPICS

1. *What do you think is in the briefcase?*

2. *Would you rather die from a drug overdose or a shot to the head?*

3. *What's more intimate: a foot massage or going down on someone?*

TWIST LIKE MIA & VINCENT

Who's got the best Twist in the room? Play Chuck Berry's "You Never Can Tell" and get ready to groove. Put the song on repeat and see who has the endurance to dance like Mia and Vincent the longest. No shoes allowed.

THE ROCKY HORROR PICTURE SHOW

A mental mind fuck can be nice. Who can argue with that?

This strange journey of a movie, complete with catchy tunes like "Dammit Janet" and "Time Warp," has become the center of sold-out movie screenings almost anywhere you go—despite the movie's initial flop of a release. For the last 30 years, fans have dressed as their favorite characters, competed in Time Warp dance contests, and of course, sung along as the movie played.

Thanks to cult classic *The Rocky Horror Picture Show*, we now know we love muscular men wearing tiny gold shorts, we wish our legs looked as good as Tim Curry's, and damn, Susan Sarandon had it going on back in the day! Let's cheers to our favorite sweet transvestite from Transsexual Transylvania and his wacky servants and creations.

Note: *If you're a light drinker, skip rules 9 and 10.*

DRINK OF THE GAME

THE ROCKY HORROR

This drink will have you saying "dammit Janet" in no time.

MAKES 2 DRINKS

3 ounces vodka

1½ ounces cherry brandy

1½ ounces orange juice

Ice

Combine ingredients over ice in a cocktail shaker. Shake well, and strain into two martini glasses.

DRINK WHEN...

1. ANYONE WEARS LINGERIE

2. **ROCKY** GRUNTS

3. ANYONE BREAKS ♫ ♪ INTO **SONG**

4. SOMEONE TALKS ABOUT EDDIE

5. JANET PASSES

6. DR. FRANK-N-FURTER HAS SEX OUT

7. ↓ RIFF RAFF & MAGENTA'S PALMS-TO-ELBOWS HAND SHAKE

8. ANYONE JUMPS TO THE **LEFT**

9. THE CRIMINOLOGIST NARRATES

10.

10. **BRAD** SAYS "**DAMMIT!**"

12. ANYONE SMOKES

13. ANYONE SHARES **INTIMATE** 👁 **EYE CONTACT**

ROCKY FLEXES

14. ANYONE DIES

15. ↘ ANYONE IS CHASED ON FOOT

16. **DR. FRANK-N-FURTER** PUTS ON OR TAKES OFF GLOVES

TRIVIA

CRASH LANDING

Ever wondered why Dr. Scott had to crash through the wall for his entrance? The set builders forgot to put an extra door in the lab set. Oops.

DINNER PARTY SURPRISE

In the dining room scene, most of the actors weren't told that Eddie's corpse would be underneath the tablecloth. When Dr. Frank reveals the body, their looks of horror are genuine.

PISS POOR ATTITUDE

The set didn't have heat or bathrooms during the filming. When Susan Sarandon requested the studio heads fix this problem, they told her she was complaining too much. She caught pneumonia soon after filming the pool scene.

BREAKING RECORDS

When *The Rocky Horror Picture Show* was released in 1975, it bombed. During opening week, Meat Loaf said he and director Jim Sharman visited a theater in the Midwest, and it was empty except for them. But in a twist of fate, as the popularity of midnight screenings spread across theaters nationwide, *The Rocky Horror Picture Show* found its audience. The movie has been shown continually in movie theaters since 1975, giving it the longest theatrical run in history.

HOT TOPICS

1. *Would you rather have a passionate evening with Dr. Frank-N-Furter or with Riff Raff?*
2. *What's the most underrated movie of all time?*

TIME WARP DANCE MARATHON

It's just a jump to the left. And then a step to the right. Put your hands on your hips. You bring your knees in tight. But it's the pelvic thrust that really drives you insane. Let's do the time warp again.

Now that you know the steps, it's time to show your moves. Who can do the Time Warp the most times in one minute? A smooch from Dr. Frank-N-Furter is the prize.

THE SANDLOT

If you've never seen *The Sandlot*, we have one thing to say to you: You're killing me, Smalls!

Everyone loves this movie about baseball and summer adventures! Whether you were an egghead, an L7 weenie, or ate your Wheaties with your mama's toe jam, *The Sandlot* reminds you of those long summer days when nothing mattered except your friends.

Summers were filled with wacky adventures, tree house sleepovers, dreaming about the hottie lifeguard at the pool, and standing your ground against the snooty rival baseball team. These are the memories that last *for-ev-er*. With *The Sandlot*, you'll always want s'more.

Note: *If you're a light drinker, skip rules 4 and 12.*

DRINK OF THE GAME

THE BABE RUTH

The Great Bambino (not the wimpy deer) was famous for drinking this combo with his breakfast.

MAKES 4 DRINKS

4 ounces bourbon whiskey

Ice

Ginger ale

Lime wedge

Pour 1 ounce whiskey into each of four lowball glasses filled with ice. Fill the glasses with ginger ale. Squeeze a lime wedge over each drink and drop it in. Stir.

DRINK WHEN...

1. Smalls's VOICEOVER

2. BABE RUTH is MENTIONED BY NAME OR NICKNAME

3. ANY MENTION OF THE BEAST

4. A BASEBALL is HIT

6. ONE TWIN REPEATS

5.

WENDY PEFFERCORN

7. "PICKLE"

8. "YEAH-YEAH"

9. THE BEAST GROWLS

10.
"YOU'RE KILLING ME, SMALLS!"

11. SOMEONE SPITS

12. INSULTS ARE THROWN

13. "FOR-EV-ER"

14. "THE SANDLOT"

15. THE GANG PLOTS AGAINST THE BEAST

TRIVIA

FRIENDS FOR-EV-ER

To establish a tight bond between Smalls and Benny, director David M. Evans had actors Tom Guiry and Mike Vitar rehearse for weeks prior to the start of filming. By the time the other kids showed up to film, they genuinely believed Tom and Mike had been friends for ages.

BIG DOG

The beast, aka Hercules, was an English Mastiff. Females tend to weigh between 120 and 170 pounds, while males are between 160 and 230 pounds.

DREAMS MAY COME TRUE

In the scene where Benny dreams of Babe Ruth, he says, "I don't know why, but can I have this?" referring to Hank Aaron's baseball card. Hank Aaron broke Babe Ruth's all-time home run record in April 1974.

HOT TOPICS

1. In your opinion, what's the best quote of the movie?

2. Squints had a mondo crush on Wendy Peffercorn. Who was your biggest summer crush of all time?

DIZZY BAT RELAY RACE

Divide the group into two teams. Place two baseball bats a distance out in front of each team. One at a time, each player will run out to the bat, stand the bat upright, and place their forehead on the bat. They will then circle the bat ten times before running back and tagging the next person in line. The first team to finish wins.

SCREAM

What's your favorite scary movie, [insert your name if it's not Sidney]?

This 1996 fright fest poked fun at the scary movie genre, while still managing to leave us jumping in our seats. But it's not all gore and guts: In the middle there's a love story. No, really. Courteney Cox, who plays do-anything-for-a-story reporter Gale Weathers, and David Arquette, the goofy and lovable Deputy Dewey, met while filming the movie and soon the on-screen love interests took their romance out of Woodsboro.

They wed in 1999 and welcomed daughter Coco five years later. Okay, fine, they finalized their divorce in 2013, but tomato, tomahto. The couple survived three additional *Scream* slasher flicks, reprising their roles for each, and hey, that's a lot longer than most Hollywood marriages last these days. Salute!

Note: *If you're a light drinker, skip rules 2, 5, and 6.*

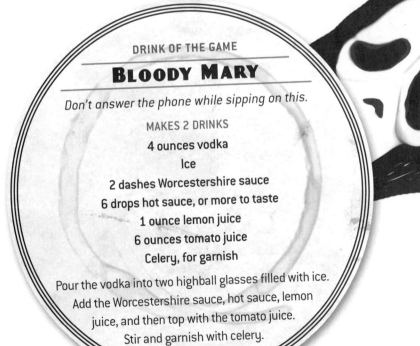

DRINK OF THE GAME

BLOODY MARY

Don't answer the phone while sipping on this.

MAKES 2 DRINKS

4 ounces vodka

Ice

2 dashes Worcestershire sauce

6 drops hot sauce, or more to taste

1 ounce lemon juice

6 ounces tomato juice

Celery, for garnish

Pour the vodka into two highball glasses filled with ice.
Add the Worcestershire sauce, hot sauce, lemon
juice, and then top with the tomato juice.
Stir and garnish with celery.

DRINK WHEN...

1. SIDNEY'S MOM IS MENTIONED

2. Scream mask

3. THE PHONE RINGS

4. YOU FEEL JUMPY

5. SOMEONE SCREAMS

6. ANY MENTION OF A HORROR MOVIE

7. SOMEONE GETS STABBED

8. SIDNEY RUNS

9. WHERE IS SIDNEY'S DAD?

10. # HORROR MOVIE RULES

11. ## THE KILLER'S VOICE

12. ## GALE DOES A NEWS REPORT

13. ## TATUM PROTECTS SID

14. ## "THE KILLER"

15. ## GALE & DEWEY flirt

16. ## GHOST FACE GETS INJURED

17.

PRINCIPAL HIMBRY

18. ## BILLY SAYS HE'S INNOCENT

HOT TOPICS

1. When was the last time you felt really freaking scared?

2. If the killer hadn't gotten to her first, do you think Rose McGowan could have fit through the garage door's pet window?

BLOODY MESS

Pull a page out of Billy's book and raid the kitchen with one goal in mind: concocting the most realistic fake blood. Bonus points if it tastes half-decent.

TRIVIA

KING OF POP CULTURE

Before creating *Dawson's Creek* and bringing *The Vampire Diaries* books to TV, Kevin Williamson wrote *Scream*, along with the following three films in the series. He makes a cameo in the second one as Cotton's interviewer.

TITLE TWIST

Scream was originally called *Scary Movie*, before, you know, *Scary Movie* and all of its spin-offs existed.

WONDER WHY

After *Scream*'s release, the use of caller ID more than tripled!

ALMOST CROSSED PATHS

Reese Witherspoon turned down the lead role, instead starring in 1996's *Fear*. Her future *Walk the Line* costar Joaquin Phoenix likewise passed on playing Billy Loomis.

BARRY SMART

Drew Barrymore was originally cast as Sidney, but she preferred the role of Casey hoping the audience would think, "If Drew Barrymore's character dies, anything is possible."

SEX AND THE CITY

Let's get one thing straight: We're only talking about the first *Sex and the City* movie here. The second one was an abomination.

Now that that's out of the way, let's reminisce. Most likely, you saw the original *SATC* flick with your besties when it came out in 2008. You felt so excited to be reunited with Carrie, Charlotte, Miranda, and Samantha. And you really wanted to know what had happened to the gals during the five years since the show ended. What had Carrie and Big been up to since we saw them get back together in Paris? How was Charlotte enjoying motherhood? Did Miranda and Steve get a happily-ever-after in Brooklyn? And was Samantha still Samantha even though she was in LA and in a serious relationship?

Some of those answers bring smiles. Some bring tears. And to get through it all, you're going to need quite a few Cosmos—obviously. So while watching this movie is a sad reminder that the show is long gone, it's also a time to enjoy and indulge in Carrie's over-the-top wedding, the gals' stunning fashion, and their nearly impossible NYC lifestyles. It's a fantasy world and Carrie's living in it.

Note: *If you're a light drinker, skip rules 4 and 14.*

DRINK OF THE GAME

COSMOPOLITAN

A drink that just might make you put a bird on your head.

MAKES 1 PITCHER (ABOUT 4 DRINKS)

1 cup chilled vodka
½ cup chilled triple sec
1½ cups chilled cranberry juice
2⅔ tablespoons fresh lime juice

Combine all the ingredients in a large pitcher. Stir vigorously for a few seconds. Pour into cocktail glasses.

→ DRINK WHEN. . . .

1. CARRIE'S TYPING ON HER COMPUTER

2. FASHION ~~~ ~~~ MONTAGE

3.  Love

4. CARRIE'S VOICE OVER

5. THE GIRLS talk about Sex

6. THE GIRLS actually have Sex

7. UNREALISTIC NYC REAL ESTATE

8. The gals drink COSMOS

9.  MR. BIG

10. MIRANDA TALKS ABOUT WORK

11. "SINGLE"

12. ANY MENTION OF MARRIAGE 💎 OR WEDDINGS

13. STANFORD OR ANTHONY —SHOW UP—

14.

GUCCI

MANOLO BLAHNIK

VERSACE

fashion designer name dropping

15. ANYONE CRIES

16.

VOGUE

TRIVIA

ROGER THAT

One of Carrie's favorite accessories in the flick? A vintage belt nicknamed "Roger" by the costume department. Sarah Jessica Parker wore the same belt in five different scenes, causing costume designer Pat Field to tell SJP to take it off because she was wearing it too often.

STRIKE A POSE

For Carrie's *Vogue* fashion shoot, the magazine's real beauty, styling, and photography teams were used. Editor-at-Large André Leon Talley makes a cameo, and off-screen, he coached SJP on how to pose *Vogue*-style.

HIGH ROLLERS

The custom couture Vivienne Westwood wedding gown Carrie receives from the designer would retail for $22,760. Drool.

HOT TOPICS

1. *Are you a Carrie, Miranda, Charlotte, or Samantha?*

2. *Fuck, Mary, Kill: Mr. Big (aka John James Preston), Harry Goldenblatt, or Steve Brady?*

3. *Would you forgive your spouse for cheating if it was only a one-time thing?*

HIGH HEEL DASH

Sarah Jessica Parker and her alter ego are pros at running in heels—even if doing so has severely damaged SJP's feet. Yikes. Now it's your turn to see if you can catch that cab or chase after your guy Carrie Bradshaw—style. Make sure to tell each guest to bring a pair of heels that fits their feet to the movie party. After watching the flick, decide on the distance of your race (like around your block or the length of your street). We suggest avoiding hills and sticking to flat ground instead. Slip on your shoes. On your marks. Get set. Go!

SUPERBAD

Remember back when you weren't 21? Ah, the days of fake IDs. While most phony names are pretty bad, McLovin is downright disastrous with a slice of awesome.

After appearing in both *The 40-Year-Old Virgin* and *Knocked Up* together, Seth Rogen and Jonah Hill teamed up once again to shine a comedic light on teenage awkwardness. And obsession with sex.

Recognize a bit of your old self in these characters? Seth Rogen certainly does. Along with pal Evan Goldberg, he started writing *Superbad*'s script when they were 13 because "we just wanted to see if we could write a movie." Yeah, sure, we were overachievers like that, too. The characters Seth and Evan are obviously named after themselves, while Fogell is a nod to their friend Sam Fogell.

Take that, Ben Affleck and Matt Damon. *Good Will* what?

Note: *If you're a light drinker, skip rules 1, 3, 7, and 17.*

DRINK
OF THE
GAME

McLOVIN-ADE

Can I see your ID?

MAKES 2 DRINKS

4 ounces vodka

Ice

16 ounces lemonade

Lemon wedge, for garnish

Split the vodka into two glasses filled with ice and top with lemonade. Garnish each with a lemon wedge.

DRINK WHEN...

1. SETH SAYS "DICK"

2. SETH RUNS

3. "McLOVIN"

4. SETH ROGEN AS OFFICER MICHAELS

5. SOMEONE GETS PUNCHED

6. SOMEONE MENTIONS EVAN AND SETH GOING TO DIFFERENT COLLEGES

7. SETH'S PENIS DRAWINGS!

8. FAKE ID

9. SETH ENDS UP ON THE GROUND

SOMEONE MENTIONS A

10. **PARTY**

11. EVAN, SETH, OR FOGELL PLOTS TO **BUY/STEAL BOOZE**

EVAN'S AWKWARD

12. AROUND BECCA

13. BECCA'S GOLD-SLICK VODKA

14. → A COP BREAKS **THE LAW**

16. EVAN OR SETH LIES TO A GIRL

17. ANYTHING **SEX-** RELATED

15.

HOT TOPICS

1. *What's the best celebrity bromance in history?*
2. *What's the craziest thing you ever did to get liquor?*

TRIVIA

F-BOMBS AWAY
The word "fuck" is said 186 times, even though *Superbad* is only 118 minutes long. For all you math geeks out there, that's about 1.6 uses per minute, with Seth alone spewing about 84 of those F-bombs. (No, we didn't count. We're taking IMDB's word for it.)

SUPER WHO?
Some theaters received prints showing the movie's title as *Separation Anxiety*.

CAN YOU SAY AWKWARD?
Christopher Mintz-Plasse (Fogell) was only 17 during the filming of *Superbad*, so his mother was required to be present while shooting his sex scene. Talk about cringe-worthy.

HEY, BRO
James Franco's younger brother Dave is the soccer player Seth yells at for peeing his pants. Like eight years earlier. Because people don't forget.

THE BEST KINDS OF FOOD ARE SHAPED LIKE…

Tap into your inner Seth and sketch your most creative penis drawings. Whoever gets the most laughs for their fine artwork is crowned the winner. BTW, writer Evan Goldberg's brother made close to a thousand penis drawings for this movie, but only a select few made the cut. So, can you put that kind of thing on your résumé?

TOMMY BOY

Full disclosure: We think Tommy was a genius to stay in college for seven years! The real world can be overrated at times (see our *Office Space* game), except on payday. Then it's awesome.

But, alas, even Tommy Boy's bubble burst when he was forced to save the family company or lose everything: house, cash, a town's worth of jobs. No pressure, dude.

This '95 classic features some of Chris Farley's best work before his untimely death two years later. Case in point: Fat guy in a little coat. The following year, real-life buds Farley and David Spade were back on the big screen cracking jokes in *Black Sheep*.

But one epic Farley flick at a time—we guarantee this one will leave you laughing till it hurts, but then we remembered what Tommy said about guarantees…

Note: *If you're a light drinker, skip rules 1, 2, and 8.*

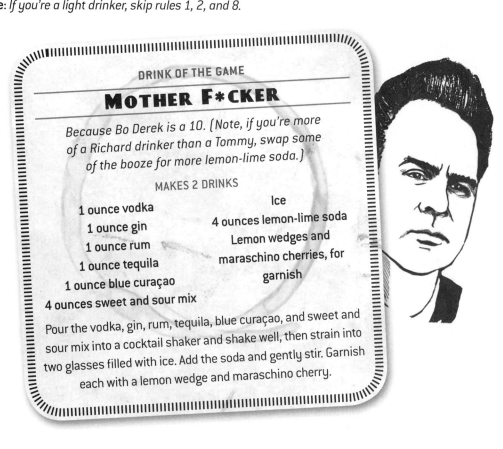

DRINK OF THE GAME

MOTHER F*CKER

Because Bo Derek is a 10. (Note, if you're more of a Richard drinker than a Tommy, swap some of the booze for more lemon-lime soda.)

MAKES 2 DRINKS

1 ounce vodka

1 ounce gin

1 ounce rum

1 ounce tequila

1 ounce blue curaçao

4 ounces sweet and sour mix

Ice

4 ounces lemon-lime soda

Lemon wedges and maraschino cherries, for garnish

Pour the vodka, gin, rum, tequila, blue curaçao, and sweet and sour mix into a cocktail shaker and shake well, then strain into two glasses filled with ice. Add the soda and gently stir. Garnish each with a lemon wedge and maraschino cherry.

DRINK WHEN...

1. RICHARD & TOMMY ARE IN THE CAR

2. Callahan AUTO PARTS ·SANDUSKY. OH·

3. ANY MENTION OF **BREAK PADS**

4. ZALINSKY

5. MANGLED CAR

6. A NEW SONG 🎵 **PLAYS**

7. RICHARD & TOMMY ⤵ GO ON A ⤵ SALES MEETING

8. SOMEONE INSULTS TOMMY

9. TOMMY GETS **HURT**

10. "Holy Schnikes!"

11. SOMEONE TALKS ABOUT THE BANK

12. "SON OF A!"

13. ROB LOWE (AS PAUL)

14. "BIG TOM"

-OR-

"TOMMY BOY"

MICHELLE

15. ♡ TOMMY

16. A CITY IS MENTIONED

HOT TOPICS

1. *If you could take a road trip with one person in the room, who would it be and where would you go?*
2. *When was the last time you went skinny dipping?*

TRIVIA

CONGRATS, GRAD
After seven years, Tommy finally receives his diploma from Marquette University, Chris Farley's real alma mater.

TOMMY LIKE WINGY
Roseanne Barr was originally set to play Helen, the waitress who Tommy convinces to open the kitchen, but her schedule was too full to take on the part.

HAIR DON'T
David Spade wouldn't allow the movie's stylist to work on his hair, hence its unkempt look.

BUTCHERING THE BUTCHER'S LINE

Who can say Big Tom's line about the butcher and a steak without messing it up? Anyone? Anyone?

WAYNE'S WORLD

Wayne's World! Party Time! Excellent!

Did you know this flick is the only *Saturday Night Live* spin-off movie to gross more than $100 million?

It's truly a babelicious movie with deep life lessons. You'll learn it's not easy to break up with crazy chicks. It's pronounced "mill-e-wah-que," which is Algonquin for "the good land." Having a flawless profile, the perfect body, the right clothes, and a great car can get you far in America—almost to the top—but it can't get you everything. And it's always funny to ask if someone in the car next to you has Grey Poupon.

Thank you, Wayne and Garth. We love you, man.

Note: *If you're a light drinker, skip rules 8 and 10.*

DRINK OF THE GAME

PARTY TIME COCKTAIL

"Hey Phil, if you're gonna spew, spew into this."

MAKES 2 DRINKS

Ice
6 ounces blended whiskey
2 ounces lime juice
2 ounces grenadine

Over ice, shake the ingredients together in a cocktail shaker. Strain into two old-fashioned glasses.

→DRINK WHEN...

1. WAYNE OR GARTH TALKS TO THE CAMERA

2. WAYNE PLAYS GUITAR

3. EXTREME CLOSE UP

4. STACY CHASES AFTER WAYNE

5. CRUCIAL TAUNT PLAYS

6. SCHWING!

7. GLEN TALKS ABOUT MURDER

8. BABE
OR ANY VARIATION OF IT

9.

Stan Mikita's Donuts

10. SOMEONE SAYS "WAYNE'S WORLD!", "PARTY ON!", OR "EXCELLENT!"

11. WAYNE'S WORLD THEME SONG PLAYS

13. QUEEN SING-ALONG

12. "WE'RE NOT WORTHY!"

14. "DREAM WEAVER" PLAYS

15. PRODUCT PLACEMENT

16. "CAMERA 1, CAMERA 2"

17.

MIRTHMOBILE

18. SOMEONE SAYS "I LOVE YOU"

TRIVIA

GOOD VS. EVIL

When he was cast in *Wayne's World*, Rob Lowe had been looking to revive his career after a 1988 video sex scandal—dirty boy! He decided to take the role as Benjamin Kane to play against type as a comic villain. The decision worked well, and he took on similar parts in *Tommy Boy* and all three of Myers's *Austin Powers* movies.

WHIP IT

In the "Bohemian Rhapsody" sing-along scene, the on-set vibe became tense between star Mike Myers and director Penelope Spheeris. "You should have heard him bitching when I was trying to do that 'Bohemian Rhapsody' scene," she told *Entertainment Weekly* in 2008. "'I can't move my neck like that! Why do we have to do this so many times? No one is going to laugh at that!'" Oh, how wrong he was!

A SPHINCTER SAYS "WHAT?"

Wayne Campbell's slang didn't always translate into foreign languages. His line, "And monkeys might fly out of my butt!" was translated into Spanish as "when Judgment Day comes." Boring!

HOT TOPICS

1. In your opinion, who's the funniest comedian (male or female) to have been a season regular on Saturday Night Live?

2. Who can do the best Wayne or Garth impression?

AIR GUITAR HERO

Every person must pick their classic rock song of choice. "No Stairway. Denied!" Create an iTunes or YouTube playlist and put the songs in a random order. When your song plays, you must perform your best air guitar. Head bang. Play like Jimi Hendrix! Show us that you're a guitar god. The person with the loudest applause (or who gets the most bras and panties thrown at them) wins bragging rights.

ABOUT THE CONTRIBUTORS

Kourtney Jason is a drinking-game expert, having played many as well as inventing new ones. In college, she wrote "*Full House* F**ked up Fun" based on the popular show's running gags—when Uncle Jesse talks about his hair was one of the rules. Today, she is an accomplished writer, editor, publicist, and overall pop-culture connoisseur. She currently dishes about celebrity relationships and entertainment for YourTango.com, and has written for MensHealth.com, Seventeen.com, and *TWIST* magazine. Her work has been featured on the *Huffington Post*, Glamour.com, and Yahoo! Shine. Jason is the coauthor of *Never Have I Ever* and author of *The Naughty Bucket List*. She splits her time between Oakland, California, and New York City. You can follow her @kourtneyjason.

Growing up in Philadelphia, **Lauren Metz** interned at the local newspaper during high school—a gig that led to her very first press badge and the opportunity to interview *NSYNC. Being that close to Justin Timberlake forever changed her life, and soon Lauren was studying at Syracuse University's S.I. Newhouse School of Public Communications. Lauren launched her career in entertainment while on staff at *Seventeen* magazine, and has since worked with numerous national media outlets, including E!, Bravo, *OK!* magazine, AOL, Alloy Entertainment, and Warner Brothers, and has interviewed everyone from Taylor Swift to Giuliana Rancic to a whole lot of Real Housewives. Lauren has also provided fashion tips for *Seventeen Ultimate Guide to Style: How to Find Your Perfect Look* and authored *The Prom Book: The Only Guide You'll Ever Need*. You can follow her @itslaurlaur.

Amanda Lanzone is an award-winning illustrator from New York. Her illustrations are seen in greeting cards, books, newspapers, and magazines, including the *New York Times*, *Popular Mechanics*, *Bitch* magazine, *Adweek*, *Juxtapoz*, and more. Lanzone earned her BFA in illustration at the School of Visual Arts, and she's received many awards and honors for her work, such as the Society of Illustrators student competition two years in a row, the SVA Alumni Society Scholarship, and the Alexander Medal at the Metropolitan Museum of Art. An avid illustrator, Lanzone has also created work for companies and won numerous art contests for brands, including Victoria's Secret and Paul Frank. You can check out her work at AmandaLanzone.com.